AF575912

293845

LEGENDS OF WARFARE

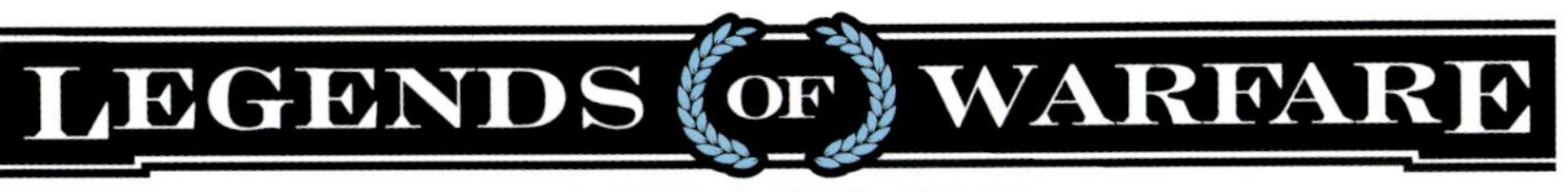

AVIATION

# B-29/B-50 Superfortress, Vol. 2

## Post–World War II and Korea

**DAVID DOYLE**

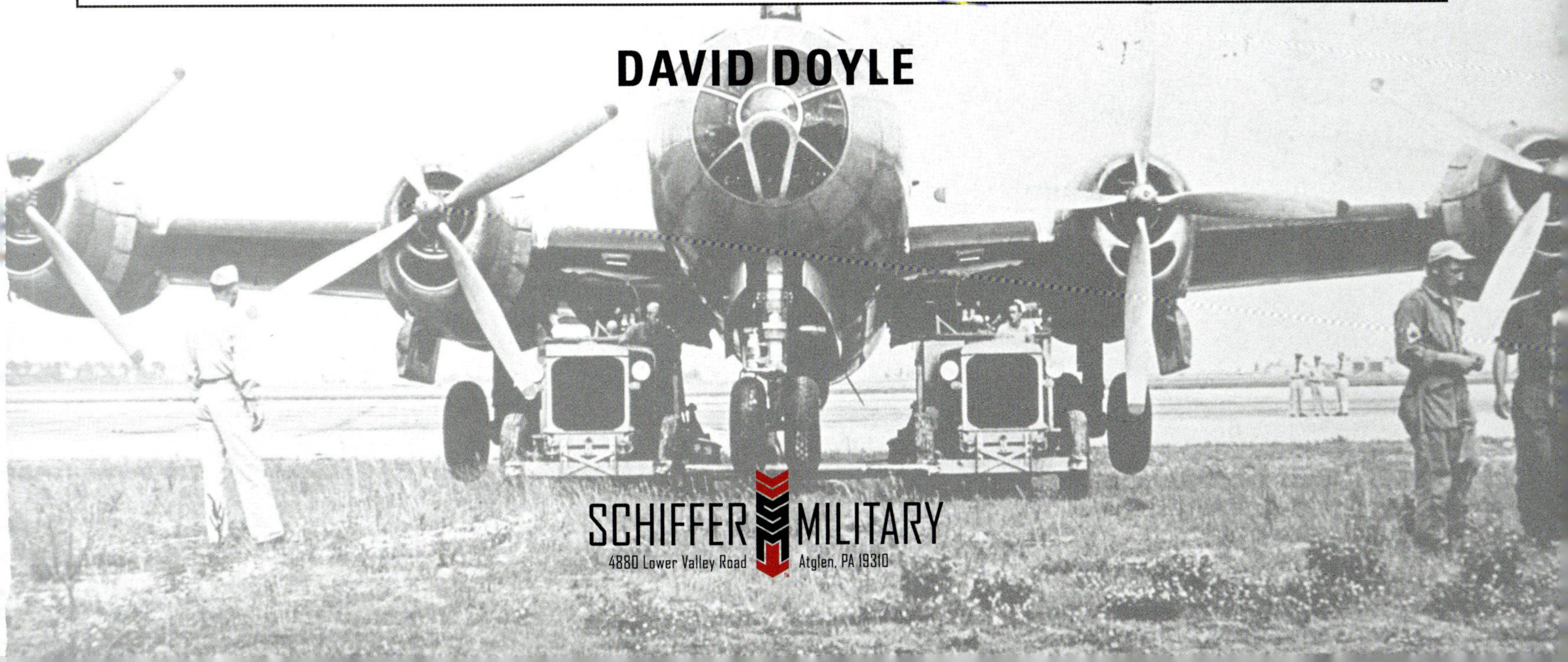

SCHIFFER MILITARY
4880 Lower Valley Road Atglen, PA 19310

Library of Congress Control Number: 2019947419



Designed by Justin Watkinson
Type set in Impact/Minion Pro/Univers LT Std

ISBN: 978-0-7643-6078-7
Printed in China

Published by Schiffer Publishing, Ltd.
4880 Lower Valley Road
Atglen, PA 19310
Phone: (610) 593-1777; Fax: (610) 593-2002
E-mail: Info@schifferbooks.com
www.schifferbooks.com



# Acknowledgments

The Superfortress had a long and storied career, meaning that trying to assemble even this concise history of the aircraft's post–World War II career required the collective efforts of many of my friends and colleagues. Among them are Tom Kailbourn, Stan Piet, Scott Taylor, Dana Bell, Bill Larkins, the staff at the San Diego Air and Space Museum, the staff at the Air Force Historical Research Agency, and Brett Stolle at the National Museum of the United States Air Force, all of whom gave of their time without hesitation.

In addition to wonderful friends and colleagues, the Lord has blessed me with a lovely and dear wife. Denise has scanned photos and pored through files beside me while doing research, and equally if not more importantly, she has been my personal cheerleader throughout the difficult parts of this project. Without her unflagging support, this could not have been completed.

All photos are from the collection of the National Museum of the United States Air Force, unless otherwise noted.

# Contents

# Introduction

As described in the previous volume on the Superfortress, development of the B-29 began in 1937. Once the US became embroiled in World War II, development and production of the aircraft took on a new sense of urgency, ultimately becoming the most expensive weapons system developed by the United States during that conflict.

The B-29 was so vital to the US war effort that multiple manufacturing facilities were employed, a topic that is covered in this introduction, even though B-29 production largely ceased at the end of the war. The end of B-29 production, however, did not mean the end to Superfortress production, since the B-50 was soon coming off the assembly line.

The three experimental XB-29 prototypes were assembled in Boeing's famed Seattle plant, but series production had to be done elsewhere, since that plant was fully involved in the large-scale production of the famed B-17 Flying Fortresses that were carrying the war to Germany.

To build the bombers that would take the war to Japan meant building new production facilities. The first of these was a government-owned, Boeing-operated plant in Wichita, Kansas. This plant, buried deep in the heart of America, not only was immune to the threat of carrier-launched attack but also accessed a labor pool not already taxed to the limit, which was the case all along the West Coast. The Wichita plant ultimately produced 1,769 B-29 aircraft.

Boeing also operated a second B-29 plant, this one in Renton, Washington, about 8 miles from the Seattle plant. The Renton plant was originally built by the Defense Plant Corporation to produce Navy patrol bombers. In time, a trade was arranged between the Army and Navy, whereby the Army got the Renton plant and the Navy got a plant in Kansas City, where North American Aviation would build PBJ Mitchells. Renton B-29 production was canceled on September 5, 1945, excepting only those already in production, a total of 1,119 aircraft.

The Defense Plant Corporation also built a B-29 plant near Atlanta. This 3.96-million-square-foot plant in Marietta, Georgia, would be operated by Bell Aircraft Corporation. Due to the proximity to the Atlantic and Gulf coasts, the plant was built almost completely devoid of windows, to allow the plant to be blacked out. Without natural ventilation, the plant was air conditioned, an unusual innovation. Today the plant produces C-130 transports.

General Motors was also contracted to build the B-29, and a plant was erected in Cleveland, Ohio, in which to build the aircraft. However, the decision was made to instead use this plant to build B-29 subassemblies as well as the P-75 Eagle fighter. During the Cold War the plant was repurposed, becoming the Cleveland Tank Plant, and built a variety of armored vehicles.

The fifth Superfortress plant, and one of four that actually assembled the massive bombers, was in Omaha, Nebraska. Built to accommodate B-26 Marauder production, manufacture of that medium bomber was phased out at the facility in April 1943 in order to convert the plant for B-29 production by the Glenn L. Martin Company. The aircraft that Martin would build were those originally contracted to General Motors.

Martin's quality control was impressive, which led to the aircraft produced in this plant being chosen to equip the nation's first nuclear-armed squadron.

Even before the United States entered the Second World War, the Army and Boeing Aircraft already were making plans for a very long-range, high-altitude strategic bomber. The prototype of this plane, the XB-29, first flew nine months after the United States entered the war, on September 21, 1942. Four plants that were part of a production pool would build B-29 Superfortresses by the thousands: Boeing, at its Renton, Washington, and Wichita, Kansas, facilities; Bell, at Marietta, Georgia; and Martin, at Omaha, Nebraska. Shown here is an example of the Boeing-Wichita B-29-25-BW, serial number 42-24464. *National Archives*

The B-29A, built solely by Boeing-Renton, had a different wing design than that of the B-29s as built by Bell, Boeing-Wichita, and Martin, being attached directly to the fuselage, with a wing-support structure installed inside the fuselage, as opposed to the B-29's wing, which passed through the fuselage. *Air Force Historical Research Agency*

Produced by only one member of the Superfortress production pool, Bell-Marietta, the B-29B was lightened by the removal of all turrets except the one in the tail, along with the fire-control computer and related equipment. This change was made possible by the reduced threat of frontal attacks by Japanese fighters in the latter stages of World War II. The twin .50-caliber machine guns in the tail turret were automatically controlled by an AN/APG-15B radar fire-control system, featuring a ball-shaped radome below the twin .50-caliber machine gun barrels of the tail turret.

Four factories produced Superfortresses: Boeing-Renton, which made only B-29As; Boeing-Wichita; Bell-Marietta; and Martin-Omaha. The Wichita facility was built by the US government in 1940 and 1941 and was designated Plant 2. Shown here are B-29s on the assembly floor.

A sense of the vastness of Boeing-Wichita Plant 2 is evident in this photo, with eight B-29s, wings installed, being in line from the plane in the foreground to the far distance. The main assembly floor of Plant 2 measured 1.7 million square feet.

Tail numbers have been applied to these Boeing-Wichita B-29s, including 26285 (representing serial number 42-6285) in the foreground and 26292 in the right background. These numbers pertained to B-29-5-BWs, the number "5" representing the production block and "BW" standing for Boeing-Wichita. Note the hinged leading edges of the inner wings, which enabled convenient access to systems in that part of the wing.

Workers at Boeing-Wichita are working on engines and accessories. In the foreground, the right wing flap is partially extended; the light-colored part of the wing above the flap is fixed. In the background, wing flaps of other B-29s are lowered to various degrees.

The 1,000th B-29 completed by Boeing-Wichita came in for special commemorative treatment, being emblazoned with signs celebrating this achievement, along with placards representing various departments of the factory, such as "SHOP 75" on the inboard left cowling and "DEPT 5A 2ND SHIFT" above that cowling on the fuselage. The Stearman Division of Boeing shared factory space at Wichita, producing the Kaydet military trainer, the 10,364th example of which is also displayed.

As production of the Superfortresses went into gear, Boeing received the use of a Navy aircraft factory at Renton, Washington, a short distance from Boeing's Seattle facilities. There, the company produced 1,119 B-29As. In the foreground of this photo is Boeing B-29A-35-BN, serial number 44-61535, while in the right background is Boeing B-29A-35-BN 44-61534.

In the foreground at the Boeing-Renton plant, the aft fuselage and empennage assembly of Boeing B-29A-45-BN, serial number 44-61802, is being moved into place, for mating to the forward fuselage aft of the wings. Hoisting cables and slings are attached to the forward end of the aft fuselage and to fittings on the aft ends of the horizontal stabilizers.

In the foreground, a forward-fuselage and wing assembly of a B-29A is under construction. With a fuselage panel yet to be installed above the wing, a part of the box-type wing-support structure in the fuselage, to which the wing is anchored, is visible. Above that opening is the left compartment for an inflatable life raft.

As seen in a photo of B-29As under production by Boeing-Renton, the pointy objects on the trailing edges of the wing flaps aft of the inboard engine nacelles are actually the tail cones for those nacelles, the bottoms of which extend to the rears of the flaps.

Women employees of Boeing-Renton are working on forward fuselage assemblies for B-29As. Atop these sections are openings for the upper forward turrets. These are pressurized compartments, with a curved rear bulkhead with a round door in the center and a round flange at the top for connecting the crew communications tunnel, which runs from the forward pressurized compartment through the unpressurized bomb bays to the aft pressurized compartment.

Under construction in this photo taken at Boeing-Renton are fuselage sections for bomb bays, with sections of crew communications tunnels in the upper parts of the sections. In the lower part of the compartments are longeron sections with round lightening holes in them.

An inspector is checking details in one of a row of engine nacelles at Boeing-Renton. The nacelles are viewed from their fronts. Visible inside the nacelles are the intercoolers, with two round openings for ducts on their upper fronts.

Bell-Marietta, located at Air Force Plant No. 6 outside Atlanta, Georgia, was one of the members of the Superfortress production pool. Here, a Cletrac is towing a newly completed B-29-5-BA ("BA" being the suffix for Bell-Marietta), serial number 42-63377, at Plant No. 6.

In the foreground of this view in the Bell-Marietta plant are various B-29 subassemblies, including a tail turret, engine nacelles, a forward fuselage section, and an empennage. Farther forward are aft fuselage assemblies with empennages installed, about to be mounted on the forward fuselage assemblies with wings installed.

In the foreground and the left background inside Plant No. 6, aft fuselage sections are soon to be mated to forward fuselage assemblies. In the right background is an airframe with the forward and aft fuselage assemblies joined together.

A center wing assembly is being hoisted preparatory to lowering it onto the fuselage section to the right. The Superfortress wings, except for those used on the B-29A, had this design of center wing, which was bolted together along its fore-and-aft centerline. Once this center wing section was installed, outer wing sections would be mounted on it.

B-29s are nearing completion on Line 5 at the Bell-Marietta factory. On the side of the nose of the closest aircraft is a sign identifying it as "SHIP NO. 279." The forward upper turret is the four-gun type. Note the sealing material over the chin scoops on the cowlings, to keep out foreign objects.

What appears to be a partially completed horizontal stabilizer and elevators assembly is on sawhorses on the Martin-Omaha factory floor. In the background is a B-29 on a conveyor. This plant came on line in August 1942; originally, Martin B-26 Marauders were produced here, with B-29 manufacturing being phased in after April 1943.

Forward fuselage sections at Martin-Omaha are nearing completion. They are on chain-propelled dollies for ease of movement along the factory floor.

Women assembly-line workers at Martin-Omaha are working on tail turret assemblies in June 1945. In the nearest turret, a woman is holding a steel bucking tool against the metal as the woman opposite her prepares to install a rivet. *GLMMAM Archive*

Forward fuselage assemblies are lined up neatly at Martin-Omaha. The nearest one has its serial number, 44-27356, and its designation, B-29-40-MO, stenciled on it below the navigator's window, below the forward, four-gun turret. Two signs are taped to the side of the nose, one reading "Combat Eagle PROJECT," and the other one, "Ship No. 297 OFF FINAL FLOOR." *GLMMAM Archive*

Pressurized crew compartments for B-29s are being fabricated in massive jigs at Martin-Omaha in June 1945. On the closer assembly are a frame of ribs and stringers and at least one bulkhead. To the rear of the closest compartment, metal skin is being installed on the frame of another pressurized compartment. *GLMMAM Archive*

Engine cowling assemblies are lined up on the floor at Martin-Omaha. To the left are extensive shop facilities, including work benches, machinery, and parts cabinets. In the background are numerous B-29s under construction.

A tubular frame attached to the nose landing gear of a Martin-Omaha B-29 is secured to two conveyor chains on tracks, for moving the aircraft along the assembly-line floor. The chin scoops of the cowlings are sealed. *GLMMAM Archive*

A stencil on the forward fuselage assembly of this B-29 at Martin-Omaha identifies it as B-29-25-MO, serial number 42-65275, with an extra suffix of "74C" following the standard serial number. The same information (but without a "C" after the 74) is stenciled toward the bottom of the next fuselage section to the rear of the forward one. Note the passage through the fuselage for the wing.

Some of Martin-Omaha's Superfortresses received glossy black camouflage paint on their undersides before leaving the assembly line, as seen on this late-production example, B-29-55-MO, serial number 44-86473. This camouflage was meant to thwart enemy antiaircraft forces during nighttime bombing operations. *GLMMAM Archive*

Martin-Omaha B-29-60-MO, serial number 44-86474 and manufacturer's number 532, is shown here arrested at the end of the final assembly line after the Army ordered the cessation of B-29 production. The final Martin-Omaha B-29 delivered to the Army was the one before this plane, serial number 44-86473. *GLMMAM Archive*

Many B-29s were placed in long-term outdoor storage after the conclusion of World War II, such as this example, which was almost entirely cocooned in four-ply plastic sheeting to protect it from the elements.

Although some of the B-29s returned to the United States after the end of World War II, many of them, particularly those at remote locations in the Pacific or that had suffered damages not worthy of repair, were unceremoniously scrapped, such as this jumble of broken-up B-29s on Tinian.

Other B-29s did not receive such extensive preservation measures as those shown in the preceding photo. These B-29s in long-term storage have had their windows covered with a reflective substance to reduce the damaging effects of high temperatures inside the planes on instruments and other sensitive systems.

CHAPTER 1

# B-29, B-29A, and B-29B: From VJ-Day through Korea

The post–World War II use of the B-29 came with considerable flourish. As the Japanese signed the instruments of unconditional surrender aboard the battleship USS *Missouri* (BB-63) in Tokyo Bay, a formation of 500 B-29s soared overhead as a show of strength. More importantly, other aircraft, with "P.O.W. SUPPLIES" painted on the underside of the wings, began a new type of bombing mission: dropping desperately needed supplies to 154 prison camps.

While war-weary B-29s were scrapped in the Pacific, fresher and newer planes continued to serve, and many were placed in long-term sealed storage.

Peacetime use of the B-29 was short lived, however. Five years after the end of World War II, Communist North Korea invaded the Republic of Korea. In response to the June 25, 1950, invasion, the United Nations, including United States forces, came to the aid of South Korea. The US nuclear-capable bomber force, including the B-50 and B-36, was too important as a nuclear deterrent to use as conventional bombers, and the chance of losing a B-36 to an enemy and the potential public-relations and security fallout meant that venerable B-29s would again see combat.

Three days into the invasion, four Superfortresses of the 19th Bomb Group, based in Okinawa, struck Communist targets. Over the next three years, B-29s of the Far East Air Force Bomber Command, based at Yokota, Japan, and Kadena, Okinawa, would bomb Communist assets. Some of the strikes were strategic-bombing raids of the type the aircraft was designed for, while others were tactical-bombing missions.

As Communist MiG-15 jet fighters began to take their toll on the Superfortress formations during daylight raids, nighttime bombing was adopted.

Although the US Army Air Force and, soon thereafter, the US Air Force, were the primary operators of the B-29 Superfortress, the aircraft was also used by two of America's staunchest allies. In 1950, eighty-seven of the bombers were loaned to the British Royal Air Force under the terms of the Mutual Aid Defense Pact.

The British used the aircraft as a temporary measure to fill the gap between the retirement of their Avro Lincoln bombers and the buildup of the new Canberra jet bombers.

The British christened the Superfortress the Washington B Mk. 1. Most of the Washingtons were withdrawn from service and returned to the United States in 1954. Two were passed along to the Royal Australian Air Force Aeronautical Research and Development Unit, which utilized the aircraft from 1952 until 1956.

However, the days of the B-29 were numbered. A few were loaned to Great Britain, providing them with a nuclear-capable bomber pending development of their own. Others were converted to serve in other roles, as seen later in this volume. However, as increasing numbers of B-50, B-47, and B-36 aircraft became available, the B-29s were scrapped or used as targets. Hundreds of the bombers littered Aberdeen Proving Ground and the Navy's China Lake Naval Weapons Center for use as targets.

Bell-Marietta B-29B-60-BA, serial number 44-84061, nicknamed "Pacusan Dreamboat," made the news headlines on several occasions during the postwar years. On November 19–20, 1945, Col. Clarence S. Irvine, deputy chief of staff, Pacific Air Command (1944–47), piloted the aircraft, unrefueled, from Guam to Washington, DC, a distance of 8,198 miles, in 35 hours and 5 minutes, setting a distance record. On the tail of "Pacusan Dreamboat" is the insignia of the Pacific Air Command. *National Archives*

Bell-Marietta B-29B-60-BA, serial number 44-84061, "Pacusan Dreamboat." On November 19–20, 1945, Col. Clarence S. Irvine, deputy chief of staff, Pacific Air Command (1944–47), piloted the aircraft, unrefueled, from Guam to Washington, DC, a distance of 8,198 miles, in 35 hours and 5 minutes, setting a distance record. On the tail of "Pacusan Dreamboat" is the insignia of the Pacific Air Command.
*National Archives*

"Pacusan Dreamboat" featured modified "Andy Gump" chin scoops on the bottoms of the cowlings; these scoops were moved from the fronts of the cowlings almost to the rear of them. The cowlings originally were designed for late-production B-29Bs. Curtiss Electric propellers were substituted for the original Hamilton Standards, and Wright R-3350-79 fuel-injected engines were installed. The tail turret was removed and a tail cone was installed in its place.

With weatherproof covers installed over the cowlings, B-29s in long-term storage are parked at the Air Material Command base at Victorville, California, in January 1946. Many of the planes have glossy black camouflage paint on the bottoms, some with wavy upper borders and some straight.

Another base where B-29s were held in storage after World War II was Pyote Army Airfield, in West Texas. A number of them are shown in this January 1946 photo. Many of the planes have identification numbers on their noses, sometimes several numbers, some of which have been crossed out with Xs.

After World War II, some B-29s made their way to Europe, such as this Superfortress with black camouflage with a wavy top, being serviced in a hangar at RAF Boreham, in Essex, England, in February 1946.

A dual-unit Linn salvage half-track is moving a disabled B-29 from the runway at Naval Air Station Patuxent River, Maryland, on June 27, 1946. The unit was able to lift the landing gear completely off the ground.

"Enola Gay," B-29-45-MO serial number 44-86292, returned to the United States after dropping the atomic bomb on Hiroshima, arriving at its new base at Roswell Army Airfield, New Mexico, with its unit, the 509th Composite Group, on November 8, 1945. The plane is seen at Roswell in March 1946, at a time when plans were for "Enola Gay" to participate in the Operation Crossroads atomic tests in the Pacific in the summer of that year. However, in the end, "Enola Gay" was not used in the tests. Nine more B-29s are in the background, none of which are wearing the arrow-in-circle tail symbol of the 509th. *National Archives*

"Luke the Spook," Martin-Omaha B-29-50-MO, serial number 44-86346, was one of the Silverplate bombers converted for use in atomic missions under the Manhattan Project, and it was a veteran of the 509th Composite Group. It is seen in the air over Bikini Atoll prior to the first atomic test there, on July 1, 1946. It had a red band on the aft fuselage and the arrow-in-circle symbol of the 509th on the tail.

"Dave's Dream," B-29-40-MO, serial number 44-27354, which had gone under the name "Big Stink" as a Silverplate bomber in the 509th Bombardment Group near the end of World War II, served as the bomber for a Fat Man-type atomic bomb in Test Able of Operation Crossroads at Bikini Atoll on July 1, 1946. The mushroom-cloud insignia of the 509th Composite Group is on the side of the forward fuselage. *National Archives*

B-29-50-MA, serial number 44-86383, was tasked with dropping a pressure gauge during the Operation Crossroads atomic tests in July 1946. B-29s involved in Operation Crossroads had the last four numbers of the serial number on the nose and the last three numbers of the serial number toward the rear of the fuselage. *National Archives*

The first of two atomic tests in Operation Crossroads was termed Test Able. At 0900 hours on July 1, 1946, "Dave's Dream," B-29-40-MO, serial number 44-27354, dropped a Fat Man type of atomic bomb nicknamed "Gilda," with a 23-kiloton yield, 520 feet over Bikini Atoll. The mushroom cloud from this explosion is seen here. *National Archives*

In a photograph taken January 12, 1947, B-29-97-BW, serial number 45-21754, is parked at Eglin Air Force Base, Florida. During that year, the national insignia on the B-29s and other USAF aircraft would be modified with red bars on the white side bars.

Boeing-Wichita B-29-97-BW, serial number 45-21754, is seen from the left front on a tarmac at Eglin Air Force Base, Florida, on January 12, 1947. The Hamilton Standard Hydromatic propeller blades are equipped with cuffs, which helped cool the engines. The cowling rings and propeller domes were painted red. *National Archives*

In the early postwar years, the relatively short range of the new jet fighters posed an urgent problem should hostilities commence, since the very long-range B-29s would be left without fighter support on extended missions. Thus, experiments were conducted with the bombers towing fighters until entering enemy airspace, at which point the fighters would be released and fly on their own. On the return trip, the fighters would reconnect with the bombers' towing apparatuses. Thus, in May 1945, P-80A, serial number 44-84995, and B-29A-10-BN, serial number 42-93921, conducted feasibility tests at Wright Field, Ohio. As seen in this photo, the P-80 had a coupling attachment on the nose for a tow cable from the B-29. After several tests in September 1947, the project was deemed unfeasible and was terminated.

In the postwar years, famed Mount Fujiyama, or Fuji, outside Tokyo became a popular backdrop for aerial photographs of Superfortresses and other USAF planes. Here, five B-29s, all of which are armed with upper and lower turrets and have triangle symbols with tail numbers enclosed on the vertical tails, are performing a flypast of Mount Fuji.

A Superfortress aircrew is lined up, receiving last-minute instructions from their commander, Col. Raymond L. Curtice, prior to taking off on the first B-29 nonstop navigational-training exercise from Giebelstadt Air Base, West Germany, to Dhahran, Saudi Arabia, in November 1947. The trip was intended to assess the reach of the aircraft. *National Archives*

After the arrival of the first B-29 from Giebelstadt at Dhahran, Col. Curtice (*left*) and his copilot, Capt. Howard Berodt, take advantage of the local transportation customs by riding on dromedaries. Note the antenna for the blind-landing equipment on the top of the clear nose. *National Archives*

B-29A-70-BN, serial number 44-62234, assigned to the 43rd Bombardment Group, is parked at an airfield about 1947. Below the cockpit canopy is the insignia of the 43rd, including a vertical bomb and the motto "READY, WILLING, AND ABLE." On the aft fuselage is the buzz number BF-234. This was a postwar identification code, with "BF" referring to the Boeing B-29 and the 234 being the aircraft identifier or Victor number. *Bill Larkins*

On Presidential Inauguration Day, January 20, 1949, six B-29s fly over the US capitol as Harry S. Truman is sworn in. *National Archives*

To achieve takeoffs of overloaded aircraft on shorter runways than normal, the US Air Force sometimes employed rocket-assisted takeoff (RATO) following World War II. Here, a US Air Force Superfortress, evidently a B-29B, is lifting off the runway at Edwards Air Force Base, California, in April 1949, with the help of an Aerojet YLR13-AJ-5 liquid-rocket motor under each wing.

| **B-29 Specifications** | |
|---|---|
| Wingspan | 141 ft., 2 in. |
| Length | 99 ft. |
| Height | 27 ft., 9 in. |
| Empty weight | 70,140 lbs. |
| Loaded weight | 135,000 lbs. |
| Power plant | Four 2,200 hp Wright R-3350-23 Cyclone 18-cylinder, air-cooled engines, each with a pair of General Electric B-11 superchargers |
| Armament | Ten 0.5 in. machine guns and one 20 mm cannon |
| Max. speed | 375 mph |
| Cruising speed | 200–250 mph |
| Service calling | 31,850 ft. |
| Range | 3,250 miles |
| Crew | 11 |

Only the last two digits, 71, are visible of the tail number of this B-29 Superfortress being towed by a tractor at an unidentified airbase in or before March 1950. In the right background are two B-17 Flying Fortresses. *National Archives*

Evidence suggests that this photo of a B-29 was taken at the same place and time as the preceding photo and may even be the same aircraft. Clear views are available of the blind-landing antenna on the nose, the Yagi interrogator antenna to the lower rear of the aft side window of the cockpit, and the flight hoods: the exhausts from the turbosuperchargers. *National Archives*

When Communist North Korean forces invaded across the 38th Parallel, thus touching off the Korean War in June 1950, the United States had just one bombardment group permanently based in the Western Pacific: the 19th. This group, based on Guam, quickly redeployed to Kadena Air Base, Okinawa, and began bombardment of North Korean targets in June. Here, a B-29 from the 28th Bombardment Squadron (Medium), 19th Bombardment Group (Medium), is being serviced at Kadena in July 1950. The insignia of the 19th Bomb Group is next to a scoreboard with fifteen bombs, indicating as many combat missions.

The practice of taking advantage of the large expanses of aluminum skin on the forward fuselages of B-29s for applying large-scale nose art, established in World War II, continued in the Korean War. One example was "United Notions," Martin-Omaha B-29-40-MO, serial number 44-27326, of the 307th Bombardment Group (Medium), based at Kadena. The plane crashed into a mountain and the crew was killed while approaching Daegu Airport, Republic of Korea, on September 13, 1951.

Following World War II, many B-29 Superfortresses were placed in long-term outdoor storage, and some of them were part of the B-29 Cocoon Project, in which parts of the airframe that were subject to sun damage and infiltration of moisture were encased in plastic shrink-wrap. In this photo dated July 11, 1946, workers at an unidentified base are cocooning B-29s, including the turrets, engine cowlings, and nose.

Almost lost in the shadows under the nose art of four black mules, each of which has a red bomb strapped to its side, is this Superfortress's nickname, "Mule Train." This was B-29-40-MO, serial number 44-86261, piloted by Capt. Glenn G. Ham from the 33rd Bombardment Squadron (Medium), 22nd Bombardment Group (Medium), based at Kadena, Okinawa, in 1950. *Stan Piet collection*

B-29 Superfortresses from the 92nd Bombardment Group (Medium) release their bombs on Communist positions in Korea in October 1950. During the Korean War, the 92nd Bomb Group used the circle-W tail symbol. *National Archives*

Visible on the tail of this B-29A-55-BN, serial number 44-62099, from the 19th Bombardment Group (Medium), is the "screaming Indian" insignia of the 93rd Bombardment Squadron (Medium). The squadron color, red, is on the nose and the tip of the vertical tail. On the forward fuselage is the sword-and-wings insignia of the 19th Bomb Group. *Stan Piet collection*

After returning from a bombing mission over Korea on February 10, 1951, two B-29 crewmen are servicing the barrels of turret-mounted .50-caliber machine guns, which are resting on a bomb stand. They are TSgt. Calvin C. Evans, *left*, and Sgt. Richard E. Fisher. In the background is the lower forward turret of their Superfortress, with the dome removed and covers installed over the gun barrels. *National Archives*

"T.D.Y. Widow" was the nom de guerre of B-29-50-MO, serial number 44-86335, assigned to the 343rd Bombardment Squadron (Medium), 98th Bombardment Group (Medium). The acronym TDY stands for "temporary duty." The victor number, 6335, is stenciled in black on the orange-colored nose-gear door. *National Archives*

Boeing-Renton B-29A-50-BN, serial number 44-61872, was nicknamed "Ace in the Hole" while assigned to the 98th Bombardment Group (Medium) during the Korean War. "DEAL ME IN" was written in red below the nose art. *National Archives*

Cpl. William E. Holder of the 19th Bombardment Group (Medium) is cleaning the bore of one of the twin .50-caliber machine guns in the tail turret of a B-29 on February 16, 1951. *National Archives*

Waist gunner Cpl. Joseph R. Harrison of the 307th Bombardment Group (Medium) checks his pedestal gunsight prior to taking off on his twentieth combat mission against Communist forces in Korea, on February 21, 1951. Cpl. Harrison had the honor of being the youngest combat crewman in the 307th Bomb Group. *National Archives*

Another B-29 gunner from the 307th Bombardment Group, Cpl. Leo J. Saunders, is cleaning one of the .50-caliber machine gun barrels of the upper forward turret in June 1951. *National Archives*

Sgt. Roy L. Annala, the central fire-control (CFC) gunner of a B-29 based on Okinawa in January 1951, is using a brush to clean the receiver covers of the .50-caliber machine guns in the upper aft turret. Behind him is the clear dome through which he operated his gunsight. *National Archives*

Sgt. John F. Graham, a B-29 gunner with the 98th Bombardment Group (Medium), is inspecting the lower aft turret at Yokota Air Base, Japan, in July 1951. Note the spent-casing ejector ports below the receivers of the machine guns. *National Archives*

Boeing-Wichita B-29-60-BW, serial number 44-69800, of the 344th Bombardment Squadron, is parked in the background as members of the 98th Bombardment Group (Medium) are unloading what appear to be 500-pound high-explosive bombs from a truck, probably at Yokota Air Base, in August 1951. *From left to right*, Sgt. Elton Cooper, PFC Donald Cunningham, a Japanese laborer, and MSgt. Dorance Stiggers. *National Archives*

Okinawan laborers watch as a B-29 Superfortress from the US Far East Air Forces returns from a bombing mission against Communist forces in Korea in August 1951. *National Archives*

Boeing-Renton B-29A-60-BN, serial number 44-62044, was assigned to the US Air Force's Tonopah Test Range when this photo was taken in August 1951. Although the nature of this plane's work at Tonopah is not understood, there are several pronounced objects that appear to be antennas or sensors on the bottom of the aft fuselage, between the wing and the aft lower turret.

Bombs with the fins installed are lined up on stands along a hardstand where "Cream of the Crop," B-29A-40-BN, serial number 44-61656, is parked. This Superfortress was assigned to the 30th Bombardment Squadron (Medium), 19th Bombardment Group (Medium). On the dorsal fin is the squadron insignia, with a rendering of "Finnegan the Cop." The squadron color, blue, is painted on the tip of the vertical tail and, in the form of a partial band, aft of the clear nose. On October 22, 1951, "Cream of the Crop" was shot down by a MiG over the Yellow Sea; the crew was able to bail out and was rescued. *Stan Piet collection*

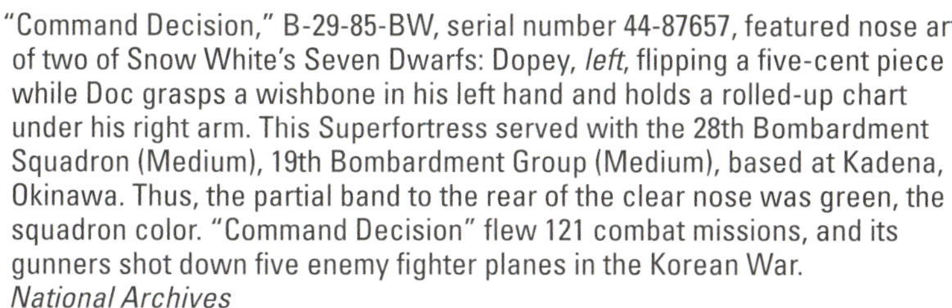

"Command Decision," B-29-85-BW, serial number 44-87657, featured nose art of two of Snow White's Seven Dwarfs: Dopey, *left*, flipping a five-cent piece while Doc grasps a wishbone in his left hand and holds a rolled-up chart under his right arm. This Superfortress served with the 28th Bombardment Squadron (Medium), 19th Bombardment Group (Medium), based at Kadena, Okinawa. Thus, the partial band to the rear of the clear nose was green, the squadron color. "Command Decision" flew 121 combat missions, and its gunners shot down five enemy fighter planes in the Korean War. *National Archives*

Boeing-Renton B-29A-60-BN, serial number 44-62103, bore the sobriquet "Haulin Ass." This Superfortress served with the 343rd Bombardment Squadron (Medium), 98th Bombardment Group (Medium), based at Yokota Air Base, Japan, in the Korean War.

Movie star Jane Russell was a hit with GIs in World War II and the Korean War, and her character in the movie *The Outlaw* had enduring appeal, as represented in the nose art of B-29-25-MO, serial number 42-65306, nicknamed "The Outlaw." This plane served with the 28th Bombardment Squadron (Medium), 19th Bombardment Group (Medium), based at Kadena Air Base, Okinawa. *Stan Piet collection*

The nose art of "The Outlaw," B-29-25-MO, serial number 42-65306, is shown close-up. The partial band aft of the clear nose was the squadron color, green.

Boeing-Wichita B-29-70-BW, serial number 44-69969, received the nickname "Beat Up Bastard," represented on the nose of the aircraft with the acronym "BUB," with the remaining letters of "BEAT" and "UP" filled in with much-smaller numbers, and the remainder of "BASTARD" covered by the blue partial band aft of the clear nose. While assigned this nickname, the plane was serving with the 30th Bombardment Squadron (Medium), 19th Bombardment Group (Medium), based at Kadena. *Stan Piet collection*

Scores of bombs are piled up in the foreground, awaiting loading on Superfortresses, while a gunner standing atop the fuselage of the B-29 in the background loads .50-caliber ammunition into the magazines of the upper forward turret. The photo was taken at an unidentified base in September 1951. *National Archives*

Framed by a B-29 parked on a hardstand at Kadena Air Base, Okinawa, another Superfortress is taking off on a daytime bombing mission against Communist positions in Korea, in November 1941. According to the original label on the photo, the plane in the foreground would soon be prepared for a mission to Korea that night. *National Archives*

Two gunners assigned to "Dragon Lady," B-29A-50-BN, serial number 44-61835, from the 30th Bombardment Squadron (Medium), pose with .50-caliber ammunition belts in front of the plane in October 1951. SSgt. Leroy Jones is to the left, next to Cpl. Claude A. Heise Jr. The scoreboard on the plane included, in addition to symbols for over eighty bombing missions, symbols for five enemy MiG fighters shot down by the aircraft's gunners. The insignia of the 30th Bomb Squadron's parent bomb group, the 19th, is on the forward fuselage, with the motto "Inalis Vincimus" ("On Wings We Conquer"). *National Archives*

Cpl. Dick Thompson of the 28th Bombardment Squadron (Medium), 19th Bombardment Group (Medium), painted nose art on several B-29s of that unit, including "Never Hoppen," B-29A-35-BN, serial number 44-61562. *Stan Piet collection*

"South Sea Sinner," B-29A-15-BN, serial number 42-93971, was emblazoned with another example of 28th Bombardment Squadron nose art. *Stan Piet collection*

Another B-29 from the 28th Bomb Squadron with large-format nose art was "Miss N.C.," B-29-55-MO, serial number 44-86376. Signs warning against smoking within 100 feet of the aircraft often were stenciled on nose-gear doors of B-29s in the Korean War, since a casually tossed cigarette butt could cause leaking aviation fuel to ignite. *Stan Piet collection*

The "Top of the Mark" on the upper floor of the Mark Hopkins Hotel in San Francisco was a favorite bar for servicemen, and the nose art of "Top of the Mark," B-29-60-BW, serial number 44-69763, was a tip of the hat to that famous lounge. The plane served with the 28th Bombardment Squadron (Medium), 19th Bombardment Group (Medium). *Stan Piet collection*

"Chotto Matte" ("Wait a Minute" in Japanese), as B-29-55-MO, serial number 44-86400, was nicknamed, is being fueled from a USAF tanker semitrailer at Yokota, Japan, on December 13, 1951. This plane served with the 344 Bombardment Squadron (Medium), 98th Bombardment Group (Medium). Shortly after taking off from Yokota on March 31, 1952, "Chotto Matte" crashed into a mountainside, resulting in the deaths of nine crewmen. Two members of the crew were rescued. *National Archives*

"Shinpaini" (Japanese for "No Worries") was a very late-production Boeing-Renton A-model Superfortress, B-29A-70-BN, serial number 44-62218, assigned to the 98th Bombardment Group (Medium), based at Yokota Air Base, Japan, in the Korean War.

Bombs are lined up, ready for loading, under "Nip On Nees," B-29A-70-BN, serial number 44-62261, with the 344th Bombardment Squadron (Medium), 98th Bombardment Group (Medium), at Yokota, Japan, in 1951. *Stan Piet collection*

To commemorate the visit of comedian and movie star Bob Hope and his troupe to Kadena Air Base, Okinawa, during the Korean War, the crew of B-29-75-BW, serial number 44-70042, nicknamed their plane "Lemon Drop Kid," after Hope's 1951 movie of the same name. The nose art replicates a scene in the movie where Hope, playing Santa Claus, takes up a collection to pay off his gambling debt. *Stan Piet collection*

"Nip On Nees" is viewed from the left side on the same occasion as the preceding photograph. The insignia of the 98th Bombardment Group (Medium) is on the fuselage, with the motto "Force for Freedom" on it. A total of twenty-one red bomb symbols indicate the number of combat missions the plane had flown to date. *Stan Piet collection*

A Superfortress takes off from an unidentified airbase on July 21, 1952, on a bombing mission against Communist forces in Korea. According to the original Air Force caption for the photo, the plane was carrying a load of high-explosive bombs. *National Archives*

Boeing-Wichita B-29-55-BW, serial number 44-69667, appears here without any markings that would identify the individual aircraft except the tail number. In addition to the "UNITED STATES AIR FORCE" marking on the fuselage, "USAF" is painted on the underside of the left wing. *Stan Piet collection*

“Sic ’Em,” B-29A-45-BN, serial number 44-61809, served with the 343rd Bombardment Squadron (Medium), 98th Bombardment Group (Medium) in the Korean War.

A 4,000-pound high-explosive bomb, mounted on a dolly on tracks, has received a paint job commemorating 252,066,000 pounds of high-explosive munitions dropped on Communist forces in the Korean War. The bomb is about to be loaded in “Sic ’Em” in August 1952. Capt. Reuben T. Long (*right*) the bombardier, and Lt. Glenn T. McClure, the radar man, are discussing the fuse for the bomb. *National Archives*

Two Japanese civilian laborers are helping unload bombs from an M29 bomb-service truck next to "All Shook," B-29-60-BA, serial number 44-84080, from the 343rd Bombardment Squadron, 98th Bombardment Group. The black camouflage paint was applied in-theater, because there is overspray on the "UNITED STATES AIR FORCE" lettering, and the crew names had been protected by masking during the painting. *National Archives*

Armorers from the 19th Bombardment Group are hoisting an aimable incendiary cluster bomb into the bomb bay of a B-29 in September 1952. During the war, an extensive fire-bombing campaign was conducted against enemy forces, facilities, and towns. Interestingly, the original Air Force caption for the photo claimed that the bomb was a high-explosive one. *National Archives*

"To Each His Own" was the nickname of B-29A-65-BN, serial number 44-62207, which was part of the 344th Bombardment Squadron (Medium), 98th Bombardment Group (Medium), during the Korean War.

"Baby San" was a Martin-Omaha B-29-45-MO, serial number 44-86290, which flew with the 98th Bombardment Group in the Korean War.

Another Superfortress assigned to the 355th Bomb Squadron in the Korean War was Martin-Omaha B-29-60-MO, serial number 44-86146, known as "Lady in Dis-Dress."

The song "Come On 'a My House" was a big hit for Rosemary Clooney in 1951, and this Superfortress, serial number unknown, presumably was named after that song. "OUR BABY" is written in red below the nose art.

The Superfortress in the foreground was "No Sweat," Boeing-Wichita Boeing B-29-80-BW, serial number 44-70134, from the 93rd Bombardment Squadron (Medium), 19th Bombardment Group (Medium), based at Kadena.

The nose art of "No Sweat," B-29-80-BW, serial number 44-70134, is viewed close-up. There was heavy wear to the red paint on the nose and on the nose landing-gear door. *Stan Piet collection*

During March 1953, B-29s of the 98th Bombardment Wing are taxiing into position prior to taking off on a bombing mission over Korea. "USAF" is painted on the top of the right wing of the Superfortress to the left. *National Archives*

The V-number stenciled on the left nose landing gear door, 9894, is the clue to the plane's identity in this May 1953 photo: Boeing-Wichita B-29-60-BW, serial number 44-69894. Crewmen are loading .50-caliber ammunition into the magazines of the forward upper turret. Pronged-type flash hiders are installed on the muzzles of the .50-caliber machine guns. *National Archives*

## B-29 and B-29A Serial Numbers

| Block number | Starting production number | Ending production number |
|---|---|---|
| **Boeing Wichita** | | |
| B-29-1-BW | 42-6205 | 42-6254* |
| B-29-5-BW | 42-6255 | 42-6304 |
| B-29-10-BW | 42-6305 | 42-6354 |
| B-29-15-BW | 42-6355 | 42-6404 |
| B-29-20-BW | 42-6405 | 42-6454 |
| B-29-25-BW | 42-24420 | 42-24469 |
| B-29-30-BW | 42-24470 | 42-24519 |
| B-29-35-BW | 42-24520 | 42-24569 |
| B-29-40-BW | 42-24570 | 42-24669 |
| B-29-45-BW | 42-24670 | 42-24769 |
| B-29-50-BW | 42-24770 | 42-24869 |
| B-29-55-BW | 42-24870 | 42-24919 |
| | 44-69655 | 44-65704 |
| B-29-60-BW | 44-69705 | 44-69804 |
| B-29-65-BW | 44-69805 | 44-69904 |
| B-29-70-BW | 44-69905 | 44-70004 |
| B-29-75-BW | 44-70005 | 44-70104 |
| B-29-80-BW | 44-70105 | 44-70154 |
| | 44-87584 | 44-87633 |
| B-29-85-BW | 44-87634 | 44-87683 |
| B-29-86-BW | 44-87684 | 44-87733 |
| B-29-90-BW | 44-87734 | 44-87783 |
| B-29-95-BW | 45-21758 | 45-21792 |
| | 45-21813 | 45-21842 |
| B-29-96-BW | 45-21793 | 45-21812 |
| B-29-97-BW | 45-21743 | 45-21757 |
| B-29-100-BW | 45-21843 | 45-21872 |
| **Bell Atlanta** | | |
| B-29-1-BA | 42-6222 | |
| | 42-6224 | |
| | 42-6233 | |
| | 42-6235 | |
| | 42-6243 | |
| | 42-63352 | 42-63365 |
| B-29-5-BA | 42-63366 | 42-63381 |
| B-29-10-BA | 42-63382 | 42-63401 |
| B-29-15-BA | 42-63402 | 42-63451 |
| B-29-20-BA | 42-63452 | 42-63501 |
| B-29-25-BA | 42-63502 | 42-63551 |
| B-29-30-BA | 42-63552 | 42-63580 |
| **Martin Omaha** | | |
| B-29-1-MO | 42-6229 | |
| | 42-6230 | |
| | 42-6231 | |
| | 42-6232 | |
| | 42-6237 | |
| | 42-65202 | 42-65204 |
| B-29-5-MO | 42-65205 | 42-65211 |
| B-29-10-MO | 42-65212 | 42-65219 |
| B-29-15-MO | 42-65220 | 42-65235 |
| B-29-20-MO | 42-65236 | 42-65263 |
| B-29-25-MO | 42-65264 | 42-65313 |
| B-29-30-MO | 42-65315 | 42-65383 |
| B-29-35-MO | 42-65384 | 42-65401 |
| | 44-27259 | 44-27325 |
| B-29-40-MO | 44-27326 | 44-27358 |
| | 44-86242 | 44-86276 |
| B-29-45-MO | 44-86277 | 44-86315 |
| B-29-50-MO | 44-86316 | 44-86370 |
| B-29-55-MO | 44-86371 | 44-86425 |
| B-29-60-MO | 44-86426 | 44-86473 |

## B-29B Serial Numbers

| Starting production number | Ending production number | Block number |
|---|---|---|
| 42-63581 | 42-63621 | B-29B-30-BA |
| 42-63622 | 42-63691 | B-29B-35-BA |
| 42-63692 | 42-63736 | B-29B-40-BA |
| 42-63738 | 42-63743 | B-29B-40-BA |
| 42-63745 | 42-63749 | B-29B-40-BA |
| 42-63751 | | B-29B-40-BA |
| 44-83890 | 44-83893 | B-29B-40-BA |
| 44-83895 | | B-29B-40-BA |
| 44-83896 | 44-83899 | B-29B-45-BA |
| 44-83901 | 44-83903 | B-29B-45-BA |
| 44-83905 | 44-83907 | B-29B-45-BA |
| 44-83909 | 44-83910 | B-29B-45-BA |
| 44-83912 | 44-83913 | B-29B-45-BA |
| 44-83915 | 44-83916 | B-29B-45-BA |
| 44-83918 | 44-83919 | B-29B-45-BA |
| 44-83921 | 44-83922 | B-29B-45-BA |
| 44-83924 | 44-83925 | B-29B-45-BA |
| 44-83927 | | B-29B-45-BA |
| 44-83929 | | B-29B-45-BA |
| 44-83931 | | B-29B-45-BA |
| 44-83933 | | B-29B-45-BA |
| 44-83935 | | B-29B-45-BA |
| 44-83937 | | B-29B-45-BA |
| 44-83939 | | B-29B-45-BA |
| 44-83941 | 44-83944 | B-29B-45-BA |
| 44-83946 | | B-29B-45-BA |
| 44-83948 | | B-29B-45-BA |
| 44-83950 | | B-29B-45-BA |
| 44-83952 | | B-29B-45-BA |
| 44-83954 | | B-29B-45-BA |
| 44-83956 | | B-29B-45-BA |
| 44-83958 | 44-83959 | B-29B-45-BA |
| 44-83961 | | B-29B-45-BA |
| 44-83963 | | B-29B-50-BA |
| 44-83965 | | B-29B-50-BA |

| Starting production number | Ending production number | Block number |
|---|---|---|
| 44-83967 | | B-29B-50-BA |
| 44-83969 | | B-29B-50-BA |
| 44-83971 | | B-29B-50-BA |
| 44-83973 | | B-29B-50-BA |
| 44-83975 | | B-29B-50-BA |
| 44-83977 | | B-29B-50-BA |
| 44-83979 | | B-29B-50-BA |
| 44-83981 | | B-29B-50-BA |
| 44-83983 | | B-29B-50-BA |
| 44-83985 | | B-29B-50-BA |
| 44-83987 | | B-29B-50-BA |
| 44-83989 | | B-29B-50-BA |
| 44-83991 | | B-29B-50-BA |
| 44-83993 | | B-29B-50-BA |
| 44-83995 | | B-29B-50-BA |
| 44-83997 | | B-29B-50-BA |
| 44-83999 | | B-29B-50-BA |
| 44-84001 | | B-29B-50-BA |
| 44-84003 | | B-29B-50-BA |
| 44-84005 | | B-29B-50-BA |
| 44-84007 | | B-29B-50-BA |
| 44-84009 | | B-29B-55-BA |
| 44-84011 | | B-29B-55-BA |
| 44-84013 | | B-29B-55-BA |
| 44-84015 | | B-29B-55-BA |
| 44-84017 | | B-29B-55-BA |
| 44-84019 | | B-29B-55-BA |
| 44-84021 | | B-29B-55-BA |
| 44-84023 | | B-29B-55-BA |
| 44-84025 | | B-29B-55-BA |
| 44-84027 | | B-29B-55-BA |
| 44-84029 | | B-29B-55-BA |

| Starting production number | Ending production number | Block number |
|---|---|---|
| 44-84031 | | B-29B-55-BA |
| 44-84033 | | B-29B-55-BA |
| 44-84035 | | B-29B-55-BA |
| 44-84037 | | B-29B-55-BA |
| 44-84039 | | B-29B-55-BA |
| 44-84041 | | B-29B-55-BA |
| 44-84043 | | B-29B-55-BA |
| 44-84045 | | B-29B-55-BA |
| 44-84047 | | B-29B-55-BA |
| 44-84049 | | B-29B-55-BA |
| 44-84051 | | B-29B-55-BA |
| 44-84053 | | B-29B-55-BA |
| 44-84055 | | B-29B-55-BA |
| 44-84057 | | B-29B-60-BA |
| 44-84059 | | B-29B-60-BA |
| 44-84061 | | B-29B-60-BA |
| 44-84063 | | B-29B-60-BA |
| 44-84065 | | B-29B-60-BA |
| 44-84067 | | B-29B-60-BA |
| 44-84069 | | B-29B-60-BA |
| 44-84071 | | B-29B-60-BA |
| 44-84073 | | B-29B-60-BA |
| 44-84075 | | B-29B-60-BA |
| 44-84077 | | B-29B-60-BA |
| 44-84079 | | B-29B-60-BA |
| 44-84081 | | B-29B-60-BA |
| 44-84083 | | B-29B-60-BA |
| 44-84085 | | B-29B-60-BA |
| 44-84087 | | B-29B-60-BA |
| 44-84089 | | B-29B-60-BA |
| 44-84091 | | B-29B-60-BA |
| 44-84093 | | B-29B-60-BA |

| Starting production number | Ending production number | Block number |
|---|---|---|
| 44-84095 | | B-29B-60-BA |
| 44-84097 | | B-29B-60-BA |
| 44-84099 | | B-29B-60-BA |
| 44-84101 | | B-29B-60-BA |
| 44-84103 | | B-29B-60-BA |
| 44-84105 | | B-29B-65-BA |
| 44-84107 | | B-29B-65-BA |
| 44-84109 | | B-29B-65-BA |
| 44-84111 | | B-29B-65-BA |
| 44-84113 | | B-29B-65-BA |
| 44-84115 | | B-29B-65-BA |
| 44-84117 | | B-29B-65-BA |
| 44-84119 | | B-29B-65-BA |
| 44-84121 | | B-29B-65-BA |
| 44-84123 | | B-29B-65-BA |
| 44-84125 | | B-29B-65-BA |
| 44-84127 | | B-29B-65-BA |
| 44-84129 | | B-29B-65-BA |
| 44-84131 | | B-29B-65-BA |
| 44-84133 | | B-29B-65-BA |
| 44-84135 | | B-29B-65-BA |
| 44-84137 | | B-29B-65-BA |
| 44-84139 | | B-29B-65-BA |
| 44-84141 | | B-29B-65-BA |
| 44-84143 | | B-29B-65-BA |
| 44-84145 | | B-29B-65-BA |
| 44-84147 | | B-29B-65-BA |
| 44-84149 | | B-29B-65-BA |
| 44-84151 | | B-29B-65-BA |
| 44-84155 | | B-29B-65-BA |

CHAPTER 2

# The Photo Birds: F-13/RB-29

The long-range and high-altitude capabilities of the B-29 made it a logical candidate for use as a photoreconnaissance aircraft, and a photoreconnaissance version of the B-29 was developed late in World War II. These aircraft were converted from airframes originally built as bombers. The aircraft were typically equipped with a trimetrogon camera arrangement consisting of three K-17B 6-inch cameras and two 40-inch K-22 cameras. Forty B-29s and ninety-seven B-29As were converted at the Denver Modification Center, becoming F-13 and F-13A aircraft. The aircraft carried the normal eleven-man B-29 crew, plus a photographer and cameraman.

The F-13 and F-13A designations did not last long. In late 1945, the aircraft were redesignated the FB-29, and then RB-29 in 1948.

When flying at 20,000 feet, the K-22 cameras in an RB-29 could photograph a strip about 2 miles wide. Two styles of film magazines were used by the RB-29 cameras, one holding 150 feet of film and the other holding 390 feet of film.

The F-13s were used extensively in documenting the results of the Able and Baker blasts of the initial post–World War II nuclear blasts at Bikini Atoll. Not surprisingly, the aircraft were also used as intended during the Korean War. RB-29s were used in peripheral reconnaissance of the Soviet Union in the early 1950s, with at least two reportedly shot down by the Russians.

In early 1944, Boeing, the Air Materiel Command, and Fairchild Camera and Instrument Company combined to develop a photoreconnaissance version of the Superfortress, with a very long-range operational capability. These planes were converted from Boeing-Wichita B-29-BWs and Boeing-Renton B-29A-BNs and were designated, respectively, F-13 and F-13A. A variety of camera suites could be installed in the F-13/F-13As, including a trimegatron camera that provided horizon-to-horizon coverage. Shown here is Boeing-Wichita F-13-40-BW, serial number 42-24583, which served with the 497th Bombardment Group in World War II.

Boeing RB-29A-55-BN (formerly F-13A), serial number 44-661960, flies above farmlands outside of Chicago, Illinois, on April 6, 1946. By this time, the plane had been assigned to the 509th Composite Group, under which, with the nickname "Mary Lou," it would soon participate with Task Force 1.5 in the Operations Crossroads atomic tests at Bikini Atoll in the Pacific in mid-1946. The F-in-square tail symbol seen in this photo pertained to very-long-range photographic aircraft used in the tests. The plane was redesignated an RB-29A in 1948, and in the postwar years it served variously with the 611th Army Air Force Base Unit, Eglin Army Airfield, Florida; the 16th Photographic Reconnaissance Squadron, 91st Strategic Reconnaissance Group, McGuire Air Force Base, New Jersey. While serving at McGuire, the plane suffered a landing accident on January 23, 1949.

Operating under the nickname "Over Exposed," Boeing-Renton F-13A, serial number 44-61999, participated in the July 1946 Operation Crossroads nuclear tests at Bikini Atoll in the Pacific. For this operation, the eight F-13As used in the tests were given extra camera stations in the pressurized compartments, turrets, and forward bomb bay. This work was performed at the Midwest Air Depot, at Tinker Army Airfield, Oklahoma City. In this view of the plane and its crew, note the canvas cover over the nose wheels, which was a standard item of issue. *National Archives*

"Kamra Kaze," F-13A-35-BN, serial number 44-61583, of the 509th Composite Squadron, is to the left in this photo taken, apparently, at Task Force 1.5's base on Kwajalein during the period of the Bikini Atoll atomic tests in the summer of 1946. This plane bears the F-square tail symbol of the photography planes. In the background are two B-29s with the B-square symbols of bomb-drop planes. *National Archives*

"Suella J," Boeing-Renton F-13A-35-BN, serial number 44-61577, was assigned to the 3rd Photographic Reconnaissance Squadron, serving as a photographic plane for the July 1946 Operation Crossroads atomic bomb tests at Bikini Atoll. The plane is seen at its base on Kwajalein next to an impressive array of photoreconnaissance cameras that were at the disposal of the squadron during this operation.

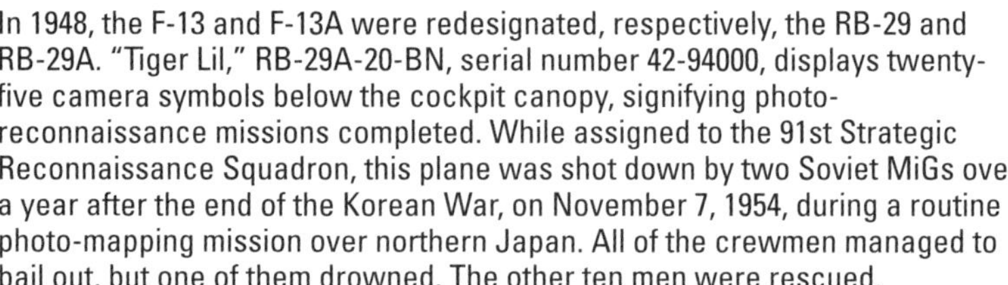

In 1948, the F-13 and F-13A were redesignated, respectively, the RB-29 and RB-29A. "Tiger Lil," RB-29A-20-BN, serial number 42-94000, displays twenty-five camera symbols below the cockpit canopy, signifying photo-reconnaissance missions completed. While assigned to the 91st Strategic Reconnaissance Squadron, this plane was shot down by two Soviet MiGs over a year after the end of the Korean War, on November 7, 1954, during a routine photo-mapping mission over northern Japan. All of the crewmen managed to bail out, but one of them drowned. The other ten men were rescued.

During August 1952, aircraft armorers of the 98th Bombardment Group, Yokota Air Field, Japan, are preparing to load .50-caliber ammunition into the turrets of an RB-29A photoreconnaissance plane. Apparently, the undersides of the plane recently had been painted glossy black, for nighttime camouflage purposes, and areas that were masked around the national insignia, the side camera window, and the emergency rescue markings just aft of the crew door remain natural metal. *National Archives*

"'Margie's Mad Greek!' III" was the nickname painted in a light color on the black camouflage paint on the forward fuselage of Boeing-Renton RB-29A-50-BN, serial number 44-61843. This very long-range photoreconnaissance plane, which still had the original turrets, served with the 31st Strategic Reconnaissance Squadron, 71st Strategic Reconnaissance Group, during the Korean War.

CHAPTER 3

# Rescue Aircraft: SB-29

The B-29 was initially adapted for use as air-sea rescue as early as 1944. However, it was not until 1949 that series adaptation of the B-29 began. Research indicates that twenty-five of the bombers were converted to SB-29 air-sea rescue configuration at Tinker Air Force Base in 1949.

The conversion involved far more than just slinging a boat beneath the belly of the Superfortress. The modifications included moving the AN/APQ-13 radome to the former forward turret position, and the radio operator's position to the waist compartment. Beneath the bomber was hung a Higgins A-1 27-foot air-droppable rescue boat.

Made of aluminum, these boats were equipped with an inboard engine and when dropped had enough fuel aboard for a 500-mile voyage. Additionally, a sail was furnished, as well as enough rations to provide for twelve men for a 1,500-mile trip.

The boats were equipped with twenty watertight compartments along with bow and stern rubberized-fabric self-righting chambers, and a self-draining cockpit. The self-righting chambers inflated automatically, ensuring not just flotation but also that the boats would be habitable. A full radio suite was also aboard each of the boats.

The SB-29 carried an eleven-man crew, consisting of two pilots, two flight engineers, two radio operators, a navigator, a radar operator, and three all-important observers.

While SB-29s could be dispatched to the area of an aviation or nautical disaster, during the Korean War a more proactive approach was taken, with the SB-29s loitering along the routes taken by bombers. This allowed them to be almost instantly available in the event a bomber went down.

Following the concept of the B-17H (later, SB-17) Dumbo, an air-sea-rescue conversion of the B-17 Flying Fortress, experiments were conducted with a similarly appointed Superfortress as early as 1944. The aircraft, dubbed the Super Dumbo, was equipped with a Higgins A1 27-foot air-droppable rescue boat. The Super Dumbo in this photo was converted from B-29B-35-BA, serial number 42-63672, and was photographed at the Birmingham Modification Center, in Alabama, in or around May 1945. *Scott Hochstein collection*

A Higgins 27-foot rescue boat mounted in the belly of a Super Dumbo at the Birmingham Modification Center is seen from the right rear. A horizontal stabilizer was mounted on each side of the aft part of the boat, and the right stabilizer is visible, but not very much so, in the foreground. Two small propellers are visible on the bottom of the boat. *Scott Hochstein collection*

A crewman is clearing parachute lines from the stern of a Higgins 27-foot lifeboat that has been dropped from a Super Dumbo during testing in May 1945. Note the hood on the bow of the boat, the toe rails on the deck, the grab rails on the side of the hull, and the horizontal stabilizer fin on the stern. *Scott Hochstein collection*

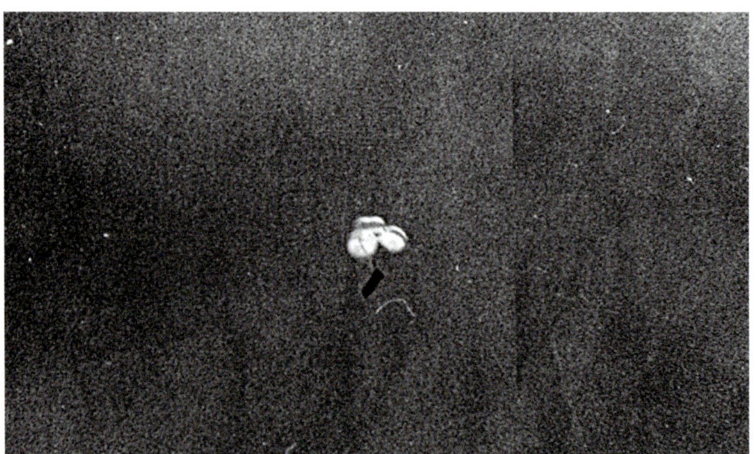

During tests for the Birmingham Modification Center in or around May 1945, a Super Dumbo has dropped a Higgins 27-foot rescue boat. Three parachutes have been deployed above the boat. *Scott Hochstein collection*

Following the successful experiments with the Super Dumbo, a small number of B-29 Superfortresses—approximately twenty-five—were adapted to the air-sea-rescue and maritime-patrol missions, with series conversions of the plane designated the SB-29 commencing in 1949. The yellow sign on the side of this SB-29 Super Dumbo indicates that it was serving with Flight C, 5th Rescue Squadron, Air Rescue Service. The Higgins A-3 EDO rescue boat was mounted bow forward. Since the boat entered the water bow-first when it was air-dropped, a heavy-duty projection was mounted on the bow to absorb some of the shock of entering the water.

The conversion work on the SB-29 Super Dumbos, which totaled around twenty-five planes, was done mostly at the Midwest Air Depot, Tinker Army Airfield, Oklahoma. The main exterior changes included the mounting of an air-droppable, parachute-equipped Higgins A-3 EDO 27-foot rescue boat; the removal of the upper and lower turrets (however, the upper and the lower aft turrets could be reinstalled for operations in combat zones); and the relocation of the radome to the front of the forward bomb bay.

The configuration of the horizontal stabilizer fins on the stern of the 27-foot lifeboat is visible in this photo of a Super Dumbo. The boat had an inboard engine, a sail, a self-draining cockpit, flotation chambers, and survival equipment and provisions.

Boeing-Renton SB-29A-40-BN, serial number 44-61671, has just released a Higgins A-3 EDO 27-foot rescue boat; a parachute is just starting to deploy above the stern. This plane is currently on static display at Whiteman Air Force Base, Missouri, and is painted to replicate one of the Silverplate Superfortresses, "The Great Artiste," which flew both on the Hiroshima and Nagasaki atomic strikes.

CHAPTER 4

# Tankers: KB-29

Two of the most important post-Worlf War II variants of the Superfortress are depicted here. In the foreground record-setting B-50 "Lucky Lady II" is being refueled by a KB-29M tanker during training mission over Arizona. *National Archives*

While World War II stretched the range of aircraft to the limits, there were times when those ranges were inadequate. In the Pacific, a campaign of costly invasions were required in order to secure islands near enough to Japan for even the long-legged B-29 to hit the Home Islands and return to base.

In the post–World War II era, a new threat to the free world appeared—the ambitious Soviet Union. The potential major Soviet targets were beyond the range of the B-29, and certainly beyond the range of the new generation of fighters being contemplated. Thus, in May 1948, efforts began to develop a hose-type aerial-refueling system.

After successful testing of this refueling system, the next month witnessed the conversion of ninety-two B-29s into KB-29M aerial-refueling tankers.

Creating an aircraft that could dispense fuel was only half the problem. Aircraft capable of taking on fuel while in flight were also required. Thus, seventy-nine B-29s were equipped with receiving equipment and designated B-29MR receivers. Additionally, all seventy-seven of the new B-50 Superfortresses extant at the time were also equipped with receiving equipment.

The reel-type refueling was complicated, requiring operators both on the tanker and receiver aircraft. That in itself precluded its use with fighter aircraft—fighter aircraft that would be essential in the event of war.

Immediately, efforts were underway to improve the refueling system. Soon, a solution was found that involved a cone-shaped receptacle on the end of the tanker's hose. With the improved system, a probe attached on the receiver aircraft was flown into the cone to make the refueling connection.

With this improvement, the system was effective and could be used by fighter aircraft, as demonstrated repeatedly during the Korean War. However, because the hose system required the operator to reach out of the aircraft, this meant that the refueling operation had to take place at low attitudes.

In an effort to improve this even further, Boeing developed the flying-boom system. First used on the KB-29P, this is the aerial-refueling system that is still used today. The flying boom is a telescoping tube with two fins called ruddervators, which work as control surfaces. Using these controls, the operator on the tanker can "fly" the boom to a receptacle on the aircraft to be refueled. Beginning in March 1950, 116 B-29s were equipped with the flying booms and modified fuel systems, becoming KB-29P aircraft.

The KB-29M was a stopgap long-range tanker for aerial refueling. Testing of the plane began in 1948, and it was fitted with a retractable hose for transferring fuel to a receiver aircraft. Along with the ninety-two KB-29Ms, seventy-nine Superfortresses were converted to B-29MR receiver aircraft. Initially, the transfer of fuel was a very laborious procedure that involved a system of cables to move the fuel hose from the tanker to the receiver plane. In this photo of "Homogenized Ethyl," KB-29M-60-BW, serial number 44-69710, the cutout on the bottom of the fuselage below the dorsal fin was for the fuel-transfer equipment. *Bill Larkins*

Because the original fuel-transfer procedures for the KB-29M and B-29MR were so complicated and impractical, a new way of transferring fuel was developed, in which the KB-29M paid out a fuel hose with a drogue on the end, which made a connection with a probe on the nose of a receiver aircraft. In this photo, a B-29 with a probe is approaching the drogue from a KB-29M over water.

With the probe-and-drogue refueling system, the KB-29M was able to refuel both B-29s and other aircraft, such as the Republic F-84 Thunderjet seen in this photo. On the KB-29M, note the truncated tail turret, the lack of upper and lower turrets, and the radome between the bomb bays.

Martin-Omaha KB-29M, serial number 44-86418, featured white, red, orange, and black stripes on the nose and tail. Three of the propellers had cuffs on the blades and were painted black, while the left inboard propeller was silver, with no cuffs.

In a photo of the left side of the same KB-29M shown in the preceding photo, a good view is available of the drogue on the fuel hose below the aft fuselage. This plane served successively with the 301st and 421st Air Refueling Squadrons.

The KB-29P tanker represented a leap forward from the KB-29M in aerial refueling, featuring a flying boom with two "ruddervators" by which an operator in the tanker could navigate the boom to a junction with a refueling receptacle on a receiving aircraft. The flying boom was of telescoping design, with a nozzle on the end. The mount for the boom was farther aft than the fuel-hose equipment on the KB-29M, and on the tail was a frame for supporting the boom when not in use. Seen here with its flying boom extended and expelling fuel is Bell-Atlanta KB-29P-45-BA, serial number 44-83951.

KB-29P, serial number 44-83907, is parked at the Oakland Airport in the early 1950s. The circle-M tail code was that of the 93rd Bombardment Group, which was based at Castle Air Force Base from June 1946 until inactivated in June 1952. The manner in which the telescoping boom was secured to the frame on the tail of the fuselage is shown. *Bill Larkins*

A North American B-45 Tornado is about to receive fuel from KB-29P, serial number 44-83927, via a refueling receptacle on the top of the fuselage aft of the wings. The square-I tail symbol of the 93rd Strategic Reconnaissance Wing is present on both aircraft.

KB-29P, serial number 42-93921, is refueling a B-29A with a highly faded exterior. The flying boom is coupled to a refueling receptacle to the front of the upper front turret on the B-29A. The boom operator in the KB-29P had a clear dome to view through on the rear of the fuselage between the branches of the boom-support frame. *National Archives*

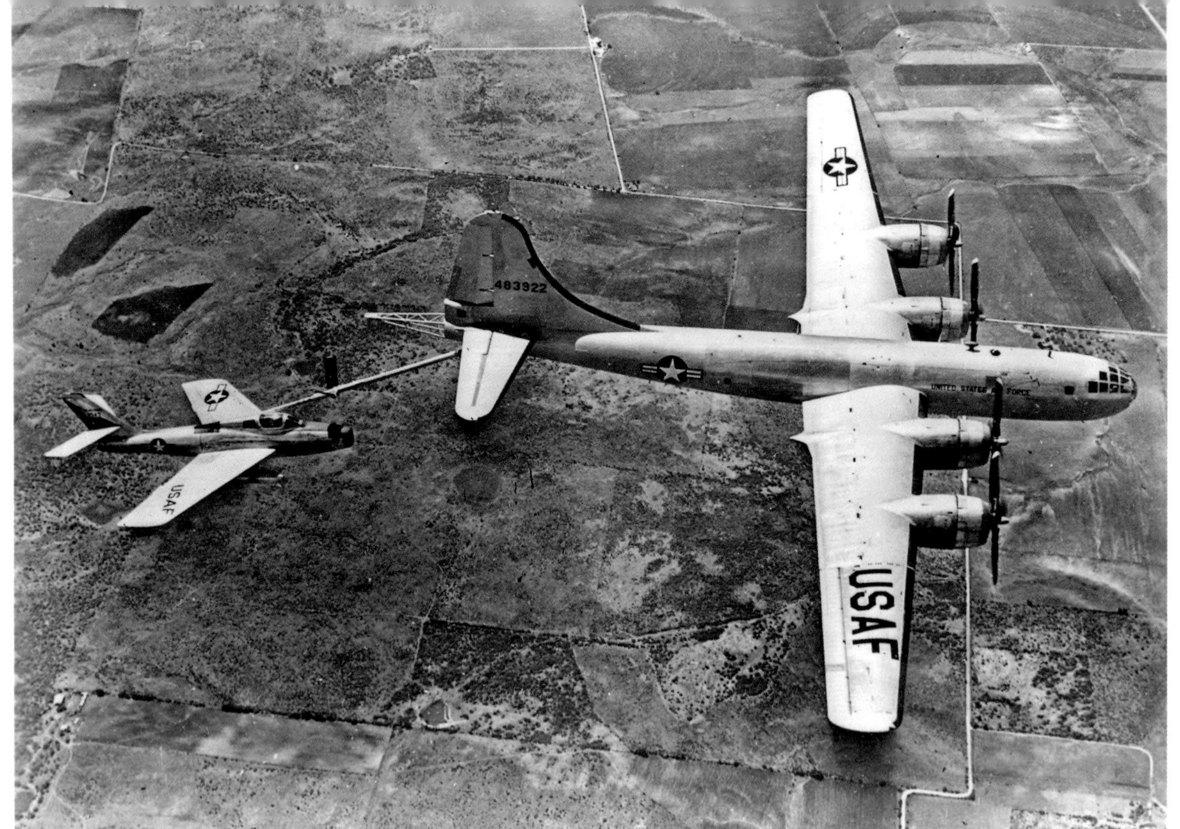


A Republic F-84F Thunderstreak is taking on fuel from KB-29P, serial number 44-83922. Further details are visible of the design of the boom-support frame on the rear of the fuselage.

A North American B-45 Tornado is being refueled by KB-29P, serial number 44-86363. Boeing-Renton converted 116 B-29s to KB-29Ps in 1950 and 1951. *Air Force Historical Research Agency*

CHAPTER 5

# Weather Aircraft: WB-29

During World War II and immediately thereafter, B-29 bombers and RB-29 reconnaissance aircraft were sometimes used for weather reconnaissance; in the late 1940s, a dedicated weather observation version of the B-29 became operational.

Designated WB-29, these aircraft were created by modifying existing B-29s. The defensive armament and armor of these aircraft were removed. Added to the aircraft were a myriad of meteorological sensors and instruments.

Although the crews of the WB-29s were given the nickname "Hurricane Chasers" because they would sometimes fly into the eyes of hurricanes and typhoons to gather information, they also had an even more ominous responsibility.

On September 16, 1947, Gen. Dwight Eisenhower commissioned the Constant Phoenix program, charging the Army Air Forces with the responsibility for detecting atomic explosions anywhere in the world.

As atomic weapons testing both by the US and Soviets increased in frequency and size, the WB-29 was deployed to sample the atmosphere for nuclear particulates.

A box-shaped projection atop the fuselage of the WB-29 replaced the Central Fire Control (CFC) gunner's dome. Called the "bug catcher" or "cracker box," this was a nuclear-particulate filter. On September 3, 1949, a WB-29 flying between Alaska and Japan detected nuclear debris from Russia's first atomic test—an event that then US secretary of defense Louis Johnson thought not possible until mid-1950.

As USAAF flight operations became worldwide in the 1940s, the collection of meteorological data became increasingly essential for operational planning. During World War II, some B-29s and RB-29s were put to work as long-range weather reconnaissance planes. In 1950, an official weather reconnaissance Superfortress was introduced: the WB-29. These were converted from existing B-29s, with turrets removed and meteorological equipment installed. This WB-29 at Travis Air Force Base, California, was converted from B-29-90-BW, serial number 45-21717. *Bill Larkins*

Flying along a coastline, WB-29, serial number 44-62225, is equipped with an orange-colored nuclear-particulate filter atop the original location of the central fire-control gunner's sighting dome. Also nicknamed the "bug catcher" and "cracker box," this filter collected air samples for analyzing the presence of nuclear particulates from US and Soviet nuclear tests. *National Archives*

A nuclear-particulate filter is clearly visible atop WB-29, serial number 42-65281, which was converted from a Martin-Omaha B-29-25-MO. This plane was assigned to the 53rd Strategic Reconnaissance Squadron (Medium) Weather "Hurricane Hunters" in the period between January 1951 and February 1954.

CHAPTER 6

# "Aircraft Carriers" and Other Unusual Variants

Experience in World War II proved that it was unrealistic to attempt to equip bombers with enough machine guns to enable them to adequately defend themselves against determined attackers. Only when the bombers were escorted by fighters could they ward off the massed assault of Luftwaffe fighters.

In the postwar era, bombers again outranged fighters. Compounding this, most fighters had only a single pilot, and fatigue became a factor. In an effort to address this, consideration was given to equipping some of the bomber force to haul the escorting fighters with them.

This was not the first time that consideration was given to using one aircraft to launch other aircraft. Prior to World War II, the US Navy airships *Akron* and *Macon* were equipped to launch and retrieve fighter aircraft.

The massive Convair B-36 Peacemaker, which was becoming America's principal heavy long-range bomber, had the capacity to carry a small aircraft. McDonnell developed the Goblin to fill this need. Referred to as a "parasite" fighter, the idea was that a B-36 mother ship would launch the Goblin when needed, and then recapture the diminutive fighter for the long trip home. The entire project was referred to as FiCon, for fighter conveyor.

In order to test the concept, Bell B-29B-65-BA, serial number 44-84111, was modified to act as mother ship during the testing of the two XP-85 Goblins (redesignated the XF-85 in 1948). The Superfortress was redesignated the EB-29B, and in order to accommodate the Goblin the aft bomb bay doors were removed and a launch-and-recovery system was installed in the bomb bay.

This mechanism, commonly referred to as a "trapeze," was lowered in order to engage a hook atop the returning fighter, allowing it to be hoisted back into the bomb bay during its recovery.

The EB-29B was dubbed "Monstro," an homage to the whale that swallowed Pinocchio in the famed Disney film.

After only a half-dozen flights in late 1948, it became apparent that this system was unworkable due to turbulence between the two aircraft, and the project was abandoned.

The Goblin was not the only aircraft launched from a Superfortress. The famed X-1, the first purpose-built supersonic aircraft, was hauled aloft for its first launch and most successive ones by an EB-29 (an EB-50 was used for some of the later launches).

The Navy also used the Superfortress as a platform from which to launch other aircraft. As of March 1947, the US Navy owned four B-29s, giving them the designation P2B. Two of these, serial numbers 44-87766 and 45-21791, were used as antisubmarine patrol aircraft and as such were further designated P2B-2S. These aircraft were assigned Bureau Numbers (BuNos) 84030 and 84031.

The other two aircraft, B-29-95-BW Superfortress, serial numbers 45-21787 and 45-21789, were given BuNos 84029 and 84028. These aircraft were designated P2B-1S and ultimately were employed as mother ships for various test programs.

BuNo 84029 was transferred by the Navy to NACA (forerunner of NASA), which used the bomber to launch the Douglas D-558-2 Skyrocket. P2B 84029, dubbed "Fertile Myrtle," would become the only airworthy B-29 ever sold to a civilian operator. Although no longer flown, the aircraft is currently owned by Kermit Weeks.

The McDonnell XP-85 Goblin (redesignated XF-85 in 1948) was an experimental parasite fighter, intended to be carried by B-36 bombers on very long-range missions to defend the bombers. The Goblin would be released from the B-36 when enemy fighters were encountered and would hook up to the bomber for the return trip to base. For testing, B-29B-65-BA, serial number 44-84111, seen in the left background, was equipped with a swiveling apparatus called the "trapeze" for carrying, launching, and recovering the Goblin. Thus modified, the Superfortress was redesignated EB-29B, the "E" prefix standing for "Exempt," a term used in the immediate postwar years usually to indicate an aircraft on bailment to an nonmilitary entity, generally for testing or developmental purposes. Seen here is the second XF-85 prototype, serial number 46-524.

The EB-29, serial number 44-84111, is taxiing with one of the two McDonnell XF-85 Goblins mounted under it. The spectacle of a large bomber with the relatively small fighter slung under it resulted in the nickname "Monstro" for the combination: a reference to the whale that swallowed "Pinocchio." Note the fixed tail skid on the EB-29.

The "trapeze" with an XF-85 mounted has been lowered during a test flight. The XF-85's wings, which were folded while being ferried by the EB-29, have been extended.

High above the Mojave Desert, the XF-85 has been released from the trapeze under the EB-29 experimental mother plane and is visible at the lower center. After flight tests revealed that the XF-85s encountered excessive air turbulence when attempting to reconnect with the trapeze, the Goblin project was discontinued.

Under the auspices of Bell Aircraft, the Air Force, and the National Advisory Committee for Aeronautics (NACA), Boeing-Wichita B-29-96-BW, serial number 45-21800, was converted to the mother ship for air launches of the Bell X-1 rocket-powered research planes. The X-1s were used in exploring the parameters of supersonic flight. Posing here in front of the mother ship is Bell X-1-2, serial number 46-063. *NASA*

The Bell X-1-2 is secured underneath the B-29 mother ship prior to a test flight in a photograph dated September 1949. The wingtip of the X-1-2 is very close to the inboard main-gear wheel. The insignia on the B-29 shows a stork that has just dropped a baby boy wielding a bow and arrow, with the inscription "BELL" superimposed. *NASA*

The Bell X-1A, serial number 48-1384, is secured in the belly of the mother ship, B-29-96-BW, serial number 45-21800. Larger than the Bell X-1, the X-1A was used in aerodynamic studies at speeds over Mach 2 (1,534.5 miles per hour) and at altitudes over 90,000 feet.

There were three Bell X-1s (originally, XS-1s): serial numbers 46-062 to 46-064. The most famous one was the X-1-1 (46-062), in which Capt. Chuck Yeager flew the world's first supersonic flight on October 14, 1947. The plane was painted high-visibility orange, and Yeager nicknamed it "Glamorous Glennis" after his wife. *National Archives*

The third Bell X-1, designated the X-1E, is being positioned under the belly of the mother ship, B-29-96-BW, serial number 45-21800, in preparation for a test flight at Edwards Air Force Base, California, during 1955. Hydraulic lifts under the landing-gear tires of the B-29 lifted the mother ship so the X-1E could be coupled to the plane. *NASA*

An X-1, evidently "Glamorous Glennis," has been mounted under the B-29 mother ship and is being fueled in preparation for a flight test in 1951. A heavy-duty sling with a D-ring at the top is supporting the forward end of the X-1. *NASA*

With a North American F-86 Sabre chase plane close below, B-29-96-BW, serial number 45-21800, is carrying an X-1 for a test flight. The part of the fuselage that originally contained the two bomb bays was cut out to accommodate the shapes of the X-1s. *National Archives*

Four Boeing-Wichita B-29s were transferred to the US Navy in March 1947. Two of them were reserved as mother ships for the Navy's experimental flight testing and were given the USN designation P2B-1S. Streaming contrails at high altitude is the P2B-1S nicknamed "Fertile Myrtle," assigned USN Bureau Number (BuNo) 84029. The plane has just released the second Douglas D-558-2 Skyrocket, BuNo 37974, a USN rocket-powered research plane. *NASA*

The second D-558-2 Skyrocket was assigned to the National Advisory Committee for Aeronautics for testing at the NACA Flight Test Center, Muroc Army Airfield, California, and was assigned NACA number 144, as seen on the tail in this photo of the aircraft being towed into position below the P2B-1S, which has been raised on hydraulic lifts. The number "127" on the tail of the P2B-1S was that plane's NACA call number. *NASA*

During 1954, a D-558-2 Skyrocket is being positioned beneath "Fertile Myrtle" inside a hangar. On the side of the forward fuselage is a scoreboard of the test flights of Douglas D-558-2 Skyrockets launched by "Fertile Myrtle," with forty-one symbols for NACA 144 (BuNo 37974), and forty-four for NACA 145 (BuNo 37975). *NASA*

One of the four B-29s transferred from the Air Force to the Navy in March 1947 is parked on a hardstand at an unidentified airfield around the late 1940s. In addition to the two planes used for flight testing and designated P2B-1S, the other two aircraft were used for antisubmarine operations and were designated P2B-2S. *Bill Larkins*

CHAPTER 7

# XB-44/B-50

As a result of the determination that the B-29's Wright R-3350 engines were underpowered for the weight of the aircraft, B-29A, serial number 42-93845, was equipped with the more potent Pratt & Whitney Wasp Major 28-cylinder, 3,500-horsepower engines, along with drastically redesigned nacelles and cowlings. Shown here, this prototype plane was designated the XB-44. It first flew in May 1945 and proved successful enough, although the original vertical tail gave the plane less than optimum controllability. *GLMMAM Archive*

The engine nacelles of the one-off prototype XB-44 had a large air scoop on the bottom for the oil coolers, intercoolers, and supercharger ram air. Four-bladed Curtiss Electric propellers were installed on the engines.

A follow-up prototype to B-29A, serial number 42-93845, was "Andy Gump," Boeing-Wichita B-29-35-BW, serial number 44-24528, named after a cartoon character without a chin, a reference to the scoops located far aft of the cowlings. This prototype also was equipped with Pratt & Whitney Wasp Major engines but also had a taller vertical tail than the stock Superfortress, to address the stability issues encountered by B-29A, serial number 42-93845. The Army Air Forces decided to press ahead with production of the plane with the enlarged tail, initially ordering 200 examples to be designated B-29D, but after the defeat of Japan this order was trimmed back to fifty planes, which were redesignated B-50A in late 1945. *GLMMAM Archive*

The very first B-50A takes shape in Boeing Plant 2 in Seattle. The massive R-4360-35 engines, the same type that would power all the B-50s, have not yet been swathed in the cowlings, but the streamlined upper gun turret is in place.

The B-50A was conceived of as a stopgap strategic bomber, capable of delivering nuclear bombs until the more advanced B-36 and B-47 bombers came on line later in the 1940s. Seventy-nine B-50As were manufactured at Boeing's Plant 2 at Seattle. The first plane off the line, B-50A-1-BO, serial number 46-2, is shown here being rolled out from the factory on June 12, 1947. In the background is Boeing YC-97, serial number 45-59592, a cargo plane derived from the B-29, with the same wings, tail, engines, and landing gear. *Air Force Historical Research Agency*

Boeing-Seattle B-50A-1-BO, serial number 46-2, is viewed from above during its rollout. "BOEING" in black type and "B-50" in red script were painted on each side of the nose of this plane. The upper forward turret had a new, semi-teardrop-shaped dome and a shape-matching fairing atop the fuselage. *Air Force Historical Research Agency*

The first production B-50A, serial number 46-2 (*left*), flies in formation with B-50A-20-BO, serial number 46-44 and buzz number BK-044. The B-50s had a new, low-profile radome on the belly between the bomb bays; on the B-50As the radome was for the AN/APQ-23A scanning radar. *Air Force Historical Research Agency*

The second B-50A-1-BO, serial number 46-3, bore the tail number 6003. The nose landing gear, which was not steerable on the B-29s, had hydraulic steering on the B-50s. The new steering mechanism is visible on the nose strut, above the dual wheels. *GLMMAM Archive*

Boeing B-50A-1-BO, serial number 46-3, is observed from the right rear. In keeping with the new, taller tail, the rudder and its trim tab were higher than on the B-29s. Four recessed hinges are visible on the leading edge of the rudder trim tab. *GLMMAM Archive*

B-50A-15-BO, serial number 46-26, was converted to a TB-50A trainer for Convair B-36 navigators and radar observers. Part of the conversion entailed removing the upper and lower turrets and installing fairings over the openings. Eleven B-50As were converted to TB-50As for the Air Training Command. As seen in this photo, on the B-50s all four of the engine nacelles extended past the trailing edges of the wings.

Nearly completed B-50As are lined up on the tarmac outside Boeing's Plant 2 in 1948. Visible tail numbers represent serial numbers 46-38 and 46-41 to 46-44. The upper and lower turrets, including their streamlined fairings, have yet to be installed. The closest plane offers a clear view of the Curtiss Electric propellers, with cuffs on the blades and spinners installed. The propellers were 16 feet, 8 inches in diameter and featured reversible pitch, to help slow the plane down upon landing. *Air Force Historical Research Agency*

Boeing B-50A-10-BO, serial number 46-17, was used as an experimental aircraft under the designation EB-50A and is seen parked at Logan Airport, Boston, on March 17, 1949. The extra radio direction-finder (RDF) "football" antenna atop the fuselage and the straight object attached to the forward fuselage above "U.S. AIR FORCE" were equipment associated with the plane's experimental work. An identical straight object also shows up on the right side of the forward fuselage in other photos of this aircraft. *GLMMAM Archive*

"Lucky Lady II," B-50, serial number 46-10, gained fame when it became the first aircraft to circumnavigate the earth. The plane, which was assigned to the 43rd Bombardment Group (Medium), took off from Carswell Air Force Base, Texas, on February 26, 1949, and, after four in-flight refuelings, returned to Carswell on March 2 after a flight of ninety-four hours and one minute. For this feat, the crew of "Lucky Lady II" were awarded Distinguished Flying Crosses and also won the prestigious Mackay Trophy for the most outstanding flight of the year. *GLMMAM Archive*

"Lucky Lady II," B-50A-5-BO, serial number 46-0010 (*lower*), is being refueled by a KB-29M, using the cumbersome cable-and-hose fuel-transfer system over Arizona during a rehearsal for the plane's history-making first nonstop aerial circumnavigation of the globe in 1949.

After its history-making circumnavigation flight, "Lucky Lady II" was flown to Tinker Air Force Base, Oklahoma, where it is seen undergoing a complete inspection by mechanics of the Oklahoma City Air Materiel Area. Before the circumnavigation flight, this plane also had received a complete reconditioning and inspection at Tinker.

"Lucky Lady II" is viewed from the right side while at Orchard Place Airport (later, O'Hare International Airport) in July 1949. Toward the bottom of the fuselage under the horizontal tail is an in-flight refueling coupler. On the bottom of the fuselage between the aft crew door and the waist observation dome are three electronic countermeasures (ECM) antennas and a blade antenna. The black-diamond symbol of the 43rd Bombardment Wing and the insignia of the Eighth Air Force are on the tail. Note the ball-shaped fire-control radome below the tail machine guns.

The second production model of B-50, the B-50B, of which forty-five examples were completed by Boeing's Plant 2 in Seattle, differed from the A model principally in its strengthened wings with lightweight fuel cells in the outer wing panels. There were other internal improvements in the B-50Bs, such as the new engine-analyzer system, which diagnosed many engine problems before they became too serious. As seen here, the first B-50B was serial number 47-118, and it first flew on January 14, 1949. Production block numbers for the B-50s ran consecutively throughout the various models, so, since the last production block for the B-50As was thirty-five (thus, the nomenclature B-50A-35-BO), the first production block of the B-50Bs came out as B-50B-40-BO. *GLMMAM Archive*

The first B-50B, serial number 47-118, was redesignated an EB-50B and was contracted out on bailment as a test aircraft. In this photo the plane has been fitted with experimental landing gear featuring bogies and continuous tracks, as part of SAC plans to deploy B-50s, other strategic bombers, and tankers to forward airfields in the Arctic regions. It was hoped that these landing gears would allow the bombers to take off and land on snowy or somewhat soft surfaces. The gear proved feasible but difficult to install and maintain, and the concept was shelved. *GLMMAM Archive*

Boeing B-50B-40-BO, serial number 47-122, was converted to an RB-50B long-range photoreconnaissance aircraft before delivery to the Air Force, following which it was redesignated an RB-50E in April 1951. The outlines of some of the camera windows are visible in this photo of the plane at Eglin Air Force Base, Florida, on October 12, 1950. Near the wingtip are two AN/APN-12A rendezvous radar receiver-transmitter antennas.

The same RB-50E, serial number 47-122, is viewed from the right rear at Eglin Air Force Base on October 12, 1950. Note the square window for a camera on the fuselage aft of the waist blister.

After completion, all of the B-50Bs except for the first one were converted to RB-50B reconnaissance aircraft. In April 1951, after delivery to the Air Force, the RB-50Bs received designations according to their missions: RB-50E for photoreconnaissance and RB-50F for photo mapping. The aircraft in this photo, serial number 47-122, was configured as an RB-50E photoreconnaissance plane. Auxiliary 700-gallon fuel tanks mounted on pylons under the outer wings were introduced with the RB-50Bs. *GLMMAM Archive*

The B-50D was the most numerous model of the B-50, with 222 aircraft completed. Its most easily recognizable feature was the redesigned bombardier's nose, comprising a single-piece blown dome with an optically flat bomb-aiming window. A heavy metal frame surrounded the bomb-aiming window. The fourth B-50D-95-BO, serial number 48-96, is seen here in flight in or around November 1949. Note the four-gun upper forward turret with the early-type dome, installed on a streamlined fairing. The use of that type of turret evidently was a result of a shortage of turrets with the streamlined domes. *GLMMAM Archive*

This view of Boeing B-50D-95-BO, serial number 48-96, was taken before the plane was delivered to the Air Force, likely on the same occasion as the preceding photo. Atop the bombardier's nose is the blind-landing antenna. *GLMMAM Archive*

**B-50 Specifications**

| **Model** | **B-50A** | **B-50D** | **KB-50J** |
|---|---|---|---|
| Wingspan | 141 ft., 2 in. | 141 ft., 2 in. | 141 ft., 2 in. |
| Length | 99 ft. | 99 ft. | 105 ft. 2 in. |
| Height | 32 ft., 8 in. | 32 ft., 8 in. | 33 ft., 6 in. |
| Empty weight | 81,050 lbs. | 80,609 lbs. | 93,155 lbs. |
| Max. takeoff weight | 168,480 lbs. | 173,000 lbs. | 179,511 lbs. |
| Power plant | 4 × Pratt & Whitney R-4360-35, 3,500 hp | 4 × Pratt & Whitney R-4360-35, 3,500 hp | 4 × Pratt & Whitney R-4360-35 + 2 × J47-GE-23 Turbojet, 5,200 lb-f |
| Armament | 13 × 0.5 in. machine guns | 13 × 0.5 in. machine guns | |
| Max. speed | 352 mph | 347 mph | 386 mph |
| Cruising speed | 212 mph | 206 mph | 219 mph |
| Service ceiling | 40,550 ft. | 40,150 ft. | 40,500 ft. |
| Range | 4,545 miles | 4,801 miles | 4,725 miles |
| Crew | 11 | 8 | 5 |

Almost the entire sweep of the undersides of B-50D-95-BO, serial number 48-96, is shown in crisp detail, including the new bomb-aiming window, the lower turrets, the underwing auxiliary fuel tanks, and the shapes of the engine nacelles. Note the somewhat flattened shape of the side of the radome between the bomb bays. *GLMMAM Archive*

In another view of the Boeing B-50D-95-BO, serial number 48-96, 700-gallon auxiliary fuel tanks are mounted on pylons under the wings. *GLMMAM Archive*

This final photo of B-50D-95-BO, serial number 48-96, is a vintage color image. Later, under the designation EB-50D, this aircraft would be converted to a mother ship for the testing of the Bell X-2 experimental rocket-powered aircraft during 1952. *National Archives*

The cranked designs of the engine nacelles are evident in this view from below of a TB-50D-70-BO trainer, serial number 48-52. Note how the wing flaps incorporated the tail cones of the nacelles. The Air Force referred to the trainer versions of the B-50 as "Flying Schoolhouses." A total of eleven B-50A airframes and eleven B-50D airframes were converted to, respectively, TB-50As and TB-50Ds for the Air Training Command. *GLMMAM Archive*

The same plane seen in the preceding photo, Boeing TB-50D-70-BO, serial number 48-52, flies high above solid cloud cover. This aircraft was assigned to the Air Training Command Bombardment School at Mather Air Force Base, California, and was used to train bombardier-navigators.

Boeing B-50D-105-BO, serial number 48-116, warms its engines at Castle Air Force Base, California, prior to taking off on a journey to the United Kingdom for temporary duty in July 1950. On the tail is the circle-M symbol of the 93rd Bombardment Wing, which was based at Castle.

A 93rd Bombardment Wing B-50D-90-BO, serial number 48-91, is being loaded for the journey to the United Kingdom on temporary duty in July 1950. These bombers and others detailed from Strategic Air Command for temporary duty at RAF Mildenhall were under the administration of the 7511th Air Base Squadron. Elements of the 93rd Bombardment Wing began arriving at Mildenhall on July 12, 1950.

A B-50 aircraft commander is giving last-minute orders to his flight crew following an equipment inspection before taking off for the first leg of the journey from Castle Air Force Base to RAF Mildenhall in July 1950. Hanging by a wire below the landing taxiing light on the nose landing gear of the closest B-50 is a small placard marked "JUDY." Note the windshield wipers on the canopy and the blind-landing antenna above the clear nose.

Boeing KB-29P, serial number 42-93921, is refueling B-50D-110-BO, serial number 49-265, by means of the flying boom over a coastline that appears to be in the Pacific Northwest. The B-50D's in-flight refueling receptacle is the wedge-shaped structure the flying boom is coupled to.

The same two aircraft portrayed in the preceding photo are seen from a closer perspective during an in-flight refueling. The operator in the tail of the KB-29P controlled the flying boom by manipulating the ruddervators: the two fins on the boom, which acted both as rudders and elevators. The ruddervators on this boom had black deicers on the leading edges.

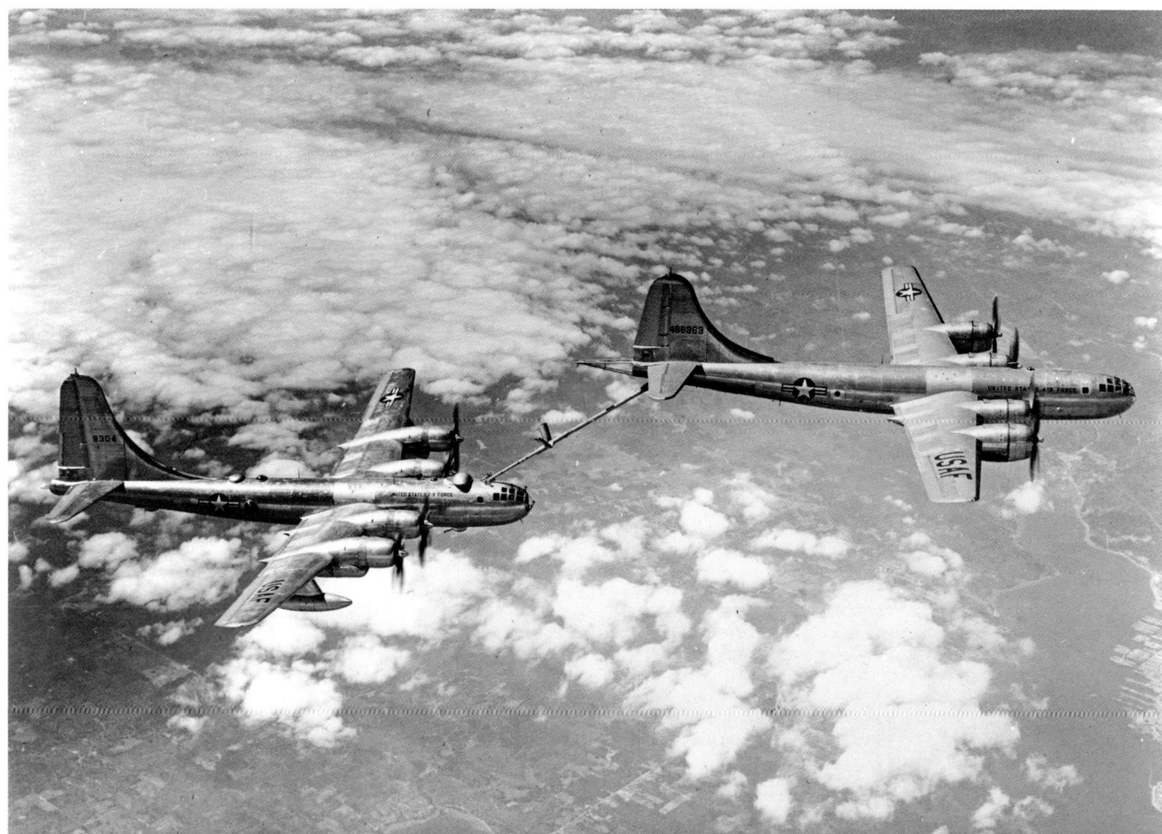


Boeing B-50D-115-BO, serial number 49-304, is receiving a refueling from the flying boom of KB-29P, serial number 44-86363. The photo dates to no later than July 1950. At some point, this B-50D was converted to a WB-50D long-range weather-reconnaissance aircraft.

B-50D-50-BO, serial number 48-101, from the 342nd Bombardment Squadron, is parked adjacent to an airport terminal, reportedly the Detroit-Wayne Municipal Airport in 1953, for display in an airshow. The triangle-O tail symbol pertained to the 97th Bombardment Group; below the symbol on the dorsal fin is the insignia of the Eighth Air Force.

The same aircraft shown in the preceding photo, B-50D-50-BO, serial number 48-101, is viewed from the left rear at an unidentified airfield. In the left background is a North American RB-45C.

In the tradition of naming some B-50s in the 97th Bombardment Wing after American cities, B-50D-95-BO, serial number 48-95, was nicknamed "City of Milwaukee." In this photo, the plane is parked at Detroit-Wayne Metropolitan Airport in 1954. The insignia of the 97th Bombardment Group is on the forward fuselage.

B-50D-110-BO, serial number 49-290, when reclassified as an EB-50D, was used as a launch platform for Northrop Q-4 supersonic target drones in the 1950s. The plane was photographed at Davis-Monthan Air Force Base, Arizona, in 1964. *GLMMAM Archive*

CHAPTER 8

# RB-50 Reconnaissance

Mechanics are performing maintenance on the left outboard engine of one of twenty-eight B-50Bs (serial number 47-132) converted to RB-50Bs by Boeing-Wichita immediately upon acceptance. Further, following acceptance by the Air Force, this plane was one of fourteen RB-50Bs redesignated RB-50E strategic photoreconnaissance planes, in April 1951. In some cases the RB-50Es were outfitted with SHORAN navigation radar on removable pallets. Jutting from the fuselage aft of the tail skid on this plane and the one in the background are the receiving couplers for the cable-and-hose refueling system. *GLMMAM Archive*

Boeing B-50B-40-BO, serial number 47-122, was converted to an RB-50E and subsequently to an RB-50F long-range photo-mapping aircraft, serving with the 1370th Photo-Mapping Group. On the tail is the "APCS" marking for the Air Photographic and Charting Service.

Built as a B-50B-50-BO, serial number 47-140, was converted to an RB-50F photo-mapping plane equipped with navigational radar. It is seen at Keflavik Airport, Iceland, in August 1956, while participating with Aerial Survey Team No. 2, 1370th Photo-Mapping Group, in Project Hiran: an electronic aerial survey. The APCS marking representing the Air Photographic and Charting Service is on the vertical tail. The tail number, 7140, is repeated on the nose landing-gear door.

The nickname “Mack’s Effort” is painted in red on the forward fuselage of RB-50F, serial number 47-144. The empennage and wings received a treatment of red paint applied to USAF aircraft that operated frequently in Arctic areas, for high visibility.

"Mack's Effort" is viewed from a higher angle, showing in more detail the application of the red paint, which was cut in around the national insignia and the "USAF" marking on the wing. The rudder and the elevators were not painted red.

"Mack's Effort" is flying in formation with another B-50B or derivative, which is not painted with the red areas. Note the dark-colored thunderbolt pattern on the 700-gallon auxiliary fuel tank on the wing of "Mack's Effort."

Boeing RB-50F, serial number 47-141, is preparing for takeoff at Forbes Air Force Base, Kansas, in early 1953. The plane was serving with the 338th Strategic Reconnaissance Squadron, 55th Strategic Reconnaissance Wing. The circle-V symbol on the tail was black, while the lightning bolts on the tail and the drop tanks were gloss insignia blue with yellowish-orange shadowing.

The same RB-50F shown in the preceding photo, serial number 47-141, is depicted ten years later, in 1963, flying low over water. At this time the plane was conducting geodetic surveying with the MATS Air Photographic and Charting Service. *GLMMAM Archive*

CHAPTER 9

# EB-50

Eighteen B-50Ds were modified for testing or other purposes and redesignated EB-50D, the "E" prefix indicating they were exempt from compliance except for Immediate and Urgent Action Time Compliance Technical Orders. Shown here at Edwards Air Force Base is EB-50D, serial number 48-96, which served as a mother ship for air-launch testing of the Bell X-2. The EB-50D has been raised on hydraulic lifts for loading the X-2 prior to the rocket-powered plane's first glide flight, in June 1952.

Boeing EB-50D, serial number 48-96, is carrying a Bell X-2 aloft during testing of the experimental rocket-powered craft. The tail turret was disarmed, and a solid, dome-shaped fairing was installed on it.

An EB-50D is transporting Bell XGAM-63 RASCAL (RAdar SCAnning Link) missile aloft around or prior to early March 1956. The RASCAL was intended to be the US Air Force's first nuclear standoff weapon; that is, an air-launched guided missile with a nuclear warhead. The RASCAL became operational in October 1957, but the program was terminated less than a year later.

Boeing EB-50D, serial number 48-75, is about to release a RASCAL. This was one of two EB-50Ds converted to carrier-director planes for the testing of the RASCAL, the other being serial number 48-111. Note the radome on the belly of the EB-50D to the front of the RASCAL.

CHAPTER 10

# Weather Aircraft

The Air Weather Service, part of the Military Air Transport Service, performed worldwide weather reconnaissance as well as collection of evidence of Soviet nuclear testing. With its fleet of WB-29 weather-reconnaissance planes becoming obsolete, the AWS procured seventy-five Boeing WB-50Ds beginning in November 1955. Lockheed Air Service performed the conversions. The WB-50Ds had all offensive and defensive weapons equipment removed, and among numerous other modifications were provisions for an airborne weather reconnaissance officer's station in the nose, as well as stations for weather observers. Depicted here in 1957 at Ladd Field, Alaska, is WB-50D 48-115, with "WEATHER" marked on the vertical tail, assigned to the 58th Weather Reconnaissance Squadron. *GLMMAM Archive*

Informational displays are set up around WB-50D, serial number 58-115, at an open house at Ladd Field, Alaska, in 1957. At the time, the plane was based at Eielson Air Force Base, Alaska. Atop the fuselage in the location of the former CFC gunner's blister is an E-1 sampling scoop, for collecting air samples to detect evidence of nuclear testing. Under the wings were F-50 sampling pods, also for testing air for nuclear particulates. These pods were converted from 700-gallon auxiliary fuel tanks. *GLMMAM Archive*

A side view of WB-50D, serial number 48-115, at Ladd Field in 1957, shows the E-1 sampling scoop atop the aft fuselage and the left F-50 sampling pod under the wing. *GLMMAM Archive*

A final photo of the WB-50D at Ladd Field in 1957 shows the weather-reconnaissance plane from the left rear. A the time, this aircraft was tasked with collecting evidence of Soviet nuclear tests both along Ptarmigan Track (Eielson Air Force Base to the North Pole) and Loon Track (Eielson to Japan). Note the MATS emblem aft of the national insignia.

In an undated photograph, a Boeing WB-50D, serial number 59-370, from the 59th Weather Reconnaissance Squadron "Hurricane Hunters," is being prepared for takeoff from Kindley Air Base, Bermuda, on a hurricane-tracking mission. The insignia of the squadron is near the nose, consisting of the meteorological symbol of the hurricane with hurricane-warning flags superimposed. *National Archives*

Boeing WB-50D, serial number 48-60, assigned to the 53rd Weather Reconnaissance Squadron, rests on a hardstand at RAF Alconbury in May 1959. The fuselage top was painted white to help cool the interior.

WB-50D, serial number 49-275, from the 53rd Weather Reconnaissance Squadron, has made a stop at Logan Airport, Boston, around 1957, en route from its home base at the time, RAF Burtonwood, to Birmingham, Alabama, where it is due to be overhauled by Hayes Aircraft. The last four digits of the tail number, 0275, are in a hexagon on the nose-gear door.

Following service with three bombardment wings in succession (the 2nd, 509th, and 97th), B-50D 49-310 was converted to a WB-50D by Lockheed Air Service, Ontario, California, in late 1956. In that guise, the plane served with the 57th Weather Reconnaissance Squadron and the 56th Weather Squadron. This aircraft is now on display at the National Museum of the United States Air Force.

Based at Yokota Air Base, Japan, the 56th Weather Reconnaissance Squadron provided weather-warning services and testing for nuclear particulates in the Far East. This WB-50D, serial number 48-108, served with the 56th WRS and is shown during a mission in 1964. Note the E-1 air-sampling scoop atop the aft fuselage and the two LP-21-LM radio direction-finder (RDF) "football" antennas on the forward fuselage. *National Archives*

The Museum of the United States Air Force, at Wright-Patterson Air Force Base, Ohio, preserves Boeing WB-50D, serial number 49-310, on static display. The aircraft is painted in an Air Weather Service scheme. Inside the clear nose in the former bombardier's station was the weather observer's station.

A wide-angle view of WB-50D, serial number 49-310, incorporates the two right engine nacelles and propellers, and the forward fuselage. From the 1960s onward, it was common for the spinners to be removed on Air Weather Service WB-50Ds. The propeller blades incorporated a black-colored electric deicer, overlaid with a lighter-colored anti-erosion shield.

CHAPTER 11

# B-50-Based Aerial Refuelers

Hayes Aircraft Company, of Birmingham, Alabama, converted 111 airframes to KB-50 tankers, equipped with three hose-and-drogue refueling stations: one emanating from the tail of the fuselage and one each on underwing pods mounted near the wingtips. An A-12B-12 hose reel was installed in each station. Shown here is KB-50, serial number 49-372, based on a B-50D airframe, assigned to the 429th Air Refueling Squadron, based at Langley Air Force Base, Virginia. The aircraft was flying over the Pacific near Wake Island during Operation Mobile Zebra in November 1957.

As seen in this photo of KB-50, serial number 48-123, refueling three North American F-100 Super Sabre jet fighters over the Florida Panhandle in 1956, to effect the refueling, each receiver aircraft had to approach the rear of the KB-50, accomplish a coupling between the probe on the receiver and the drogue on the hose from the tanker, and then approach within 8 feet of the KB-50 for the fuel to start flowing to the receiver.

Four KB-50 tankers are lined up at the plant where they were converted: Hayes Aircraft, at the Birmingham, Alabama, airport. The tail numbers of the first three planes are visible, and they all pertain to KB-50s converted from B-50D bombers: serial numbers 49-309, 48-81, and 49-292. The tail turrets were eliminated and revamped to house the center hose reels. *GLMMAM Archive*

Hayes Aircraft, of Birmingham, Alabama, converted eighty-five B-50D-based KB-50s and fifteen B-50Ds to KB-50J tankers, on which the two underwing auxiliary fuel tanks were replaced by General Electric J47 turbojet engines. The nickname "Queen Bee" is marked on the nose-gear door of KB-50J, serial number 49-282. *National Archives*

In an undated view of a KB-50J during a mission, the hump with the black front on the top of the aft fuselage is an identification friend or foe (IFF) interrogator antenna. The KB-50Js incorporated a new, greatly enlarged hose-reel fairing on the tail, which is somewhat visible from this perspective. *National Archives*

This undated photo of a KB-50J refuelling two F-100Ds of the USAF Thunderbirds provides a good view of the identification-friend-or-foe (IFF) interrogator antenna; the hump with the black front on the top of the aft fuselage. The KB-50Js incorporated a new, greatly enlarged hose-reel fairing on the tail, which is somewhat visible from this perspective. *National Archives*

A flight line of KB-50J tankers at Hickam Air Force Base, Hawaii, on January 31, 1965, includes serial number 48-79 (*foreground*), which started out as a B-50D and was converted to a KB-50 before being revamped to a KB-50J. The last three digits of this plane's tail number, 079, are stenciled in small numerals on the nose-gear door. The aircraft are being prepared for retirement. *National Archives*

Looking at a glance like a B-29, Boeing's B-50 was the final development of the Superfortress to enter production, and variations of the aircraft served well into the jet age, with the last being retired in 1965. The B-50 was optimized to deliver nuclear weapons. This colorful example was used by the Special Weapons Command in connection with the nuclear test program, Indian Springs Air Force Base, Nevada, in March 1953. *National Archives*